Poems
In
The
Pink

Published By TDP Publications

All rights reserved. No part of this publication may be
reproduced or transmitted in any form or by any means,
electronic or mechanical, including photocopy,
recording or any other information storage and retrieval
system, without prior permission in writing
from the publisher.

A catalogue record of this book is available from
The British Library
ISBN: 0-9548609-0-X

The right of the individual poets to be identified as the
authors of this book has been asserted by them in accordance
with the Copyright, Designs and Patents Act 1988

We are grateful to Route for their kind permission to
reproduce some poems from Psychicbread,
written by Mark Gwynne Jones.

Printed in Great Britain by
Russell Press Ltd

Cover and typesetting by Sprint Print of Newthorpe

First Published in 2004 by
TDP Publications

Poets In The Pink

This book has been my dream. And it started at Easter as I sat in the cinema waiting for the film to start. I found myself extremely moved by an advert for Tesco's Race For Life and knew that even though my running days are well in the past I had to do something to play my part in the battle against Cancer.

I have been wonderfully supported and encouraged both by the poets who have contributed so freely and generously, and by the very many people in and around Eastwood whose goodwill and enthusiasm have kept this project moving.

I am especially grateful to Steve Birch, without whom this book might never have gone beyond being a dream.

And finally, I thank you for buying this book and helping to support the work of Cancer Research UK.
Bless you.

James Haddow
Aka The Taxi Driver Poet

Poets In The Pink

CONTENTS

The Taxi Driver Poet   9

All I'll Give Is All I Am	11
Deceit In Disguise	12
Spinning Out Of Control	14
The Spinner Spun	15
Everybody's Doing It!	16
Disposable People, Disposable Lives	18
An Inch Upon A Map	20
You Are The Weakest Link - Goodbye!!	21
Why A Woman Turns The Lights Off	22
Without You	24

Louise Ashley   27

When Did You Stop Living?	29
Bite	30
In Bed With A Poet	31
Peel Me Off The Ceiling	32
Sun Goddess	34
Semper Fidelis	35
Silence	36
The Familiarity Of Your Kiss	37
Strawberries And Champagne (No Compromise!)	38
Little Devils	40
Beyond The Ironing Pile	41
Death By TV	42

Mark Gwynne Jones   43

All Tanked Up!	45
Wake The Dead	48
Plastic Man	50
Helical Staircase	52
Orange Girl	54
Cuckoo In A Clock	58
The Natterjack Toad	60

Alison L R Davies   61

Love All Consuming	63
Summer That Was	64
Tree Magic	66
On Raven Wings	67
Fran	68
Love	70
Stolen	71
Queen Of The Undead	72

Michael J Kaye   73

Honey Jar	75
How Little, How Little I Know	76
Pyrotechnics Of The Heart	78
Song Of Nothing	80
Where Is He?	84
Excess Baggage	86
Puncture	88

Michelle "Mother" Hubbard   89

Standing Out In A Crowd   91
The Travellers Prayer   92
I'm Leaving   93
Mind Your Words   94
Untitled   95
Birds Eye View   96
All Woman   98
This Lustful Affair   99
The Humble Oasis   100
My Box Of Bryant And May   101
Bee Stings   102
Prayers In The Darkness   103
Love's Maturity   104

Ian Collinson   105

I Wish I Could Write Like A Woman   107
Conversations With My Daughter   108
One Foot In The Rave   110
Nutcrackers   111
Intellectual   112
Some Of My Best Friends Are Answering Machines   114
Nearly Beloved   116
Lady Of The Rings   118

Sue Allen   119

Men Are Like Bras   121
Love In Cinemascope   122
I'm Only a Girlie   123
Heartless   124
I Want To Be Sting's Acoustic Guitar   125
You Painted Me In Pale, Pale Blue   126

Poets In The Pink

Green Hog Day	127
Broken Dreams Of Better Places	128
Black Orchid	129
Collision Course	130
Circus Act	131
St. Elmo's Fire	132
Captive Butterfly Wings	133
Isis And Osiris	134

Neil F Winfield — 135

Making Love	137
Good Women	138
The Greatest	139
Marriage	140
Suspicion	141
Impressions	141
Lunatic	141
Drink	142
Politicians	142
Pets	142
Man	143
Woman	143
Dogs	143
Rock Of Ages	144
From My Window	144

Diane Doran — 145

To Watch You Sleeping	147
Sexual Truth	148
Projections	151
I Want It This Way	152

Distant Infant	154
Help Me, Don't Help Me	155
Blue Abalone	156
Tip Top, Pucka	158

Andy Postman — 159

The ABC Applied To Me	161
Monty Don	162
Slug In A Windmill	164
And When I'm Up I'm Up	165
Brown	166
Edwood Woodwood	168
The Theory Of Everything	170

June Staines — 171

Heaven No's	173
Inferno	174
I Love It	175
Second Thoughts	176

Ken Swallow — 177

Valentine	179
Ant	180
The Kiss	181
Cardsharp	182
Diamond Days	183
Not A Poem On The Page	184
The Peak Pass Road	186
Bodger Blues	187
The Dot Com Lot	188
The Cyclist	190

~ The Taxi Driver Poet ~

James, and his instantly recognised 'poet-mobile' have become a regular and welcome sight around Eastwood where he is affectionately called 'Poet' and sometimes slightly more reverentially, 'Mister Poet'.

His repertoire ranges from affairs of the heart, to observational humour, political satire, and current affairs. If you're ever in his taxi then make sure he tells you that one about Barrymore, or Stan Collymore, or his ex-missus or . . . .

Visit him at www.taxidriverpoet.com

Poets In The Pink

~ The Taxi Driver Poet ~

ALL I'LL GIVE IS ALL I AM

If I lived with rich and famous stars
Drove fast, expensive, flashy cars
And dined with kings, and queens and tsars
In elegant exclusive bars

If I had all that money brings
Gave you the works, the full trappings
Rich, exotic, fancy things
And gold, and silver, diamond rings

If fame and fortune came my way
With treasures I can't count or weigh
Though I gave all, that wouldn't outweigh
The love I'd give to you today

All that I am and still can be,
However rich or poor I be
I'll give you unreservedly
The essence that is truly me

And I couldn't ever give you more
Regardless of my treasure store
Coz I'll give you all I am for sure
Sweet gorgeous girl that I adore.

~ The Taxi Driver Poet ~

DECEIT IN DISGUISE

Jordan's got weapons of mass distraction
Carol Vorderman's the queen of maths subtraction
Kylie's got a bum fit for mass seduction
    But we can't find weapons of mass destruction
    No, we can't find weapons of mass destruction.

Radio's the medium of mass reception
Spin doctors pouring out their crass deception
The Chancellor keeps hiking up your gross deduction
    But we can't find weapons of mass destruction
    No, we can't find weapons of mass destruction

There's a shortage of dentists doing NHS extractions
We're running out of teachers for class instruction
We've got "Doctors for refugees"- there's such an influxion
    But we can't find weapons of mass destruction
    No, we can't find weapons of mass destruction

Philosophers argue over moral abstractions
Reality TV is the new attraction
Beaming out war like a Spielberg production
    But we can't find weapons of mass destruction
    No, we can't find weapons of mass destruction

Truth is the victim - it's a gross traduction
Weapons Inspectors can't serve their function
Saddam's gone - now there's NO obstruction
    Still we can't find weapons of mass destruction
    No, we can't find weapons of mass destruction

~ The Taxi Driver Poet ~

Intelligence came from our network of spies
From beneath the waves and above the skies
But take some advice - here's a word to the wise
    Spin's just a word for deceit in disguise
    Yeah, spin's just a word for deceit in disguise

Are they serving up to you just a diet of lies
Where they slander and slur just to demonise
To justify their actions and look good in our eyes?
    Spin's just a word for deceit in disguise
    Yeah, spin's just a word for deceit in disguise

Concentrate your minds and open your eyes
It's time to wake up and to realise
"they" won't tell us wherefores and they won't tell us whys
    Spin's just a word for deceit in disguise
    Yeah, spin's just a word for deceit in disguise

They said he'd got weapons of mass destruction
That justified war and a country's destruction
Now Saddam's gone and there's NO obstruction
And still . . . .
    They can't find weapons of mass destruction
    No, they CAN'T find weapons of mass destruction

~ The Taxi Driver Poet ~

SPINNING OUT OF CONTROL

How many more innocents
Have to die
While spinners spin
And liars lie
And schemers plot
In the dark of night
To make their deeds
Of wrong look right?
Well crocodile tears
Won't purge your shame
You pass the buck
Accept no blame
For no-one stands
To take the can
You've spilled the blood
Of an innocent man

~ The Taxi Driver Poet ~

THE SPINNER SPUN

Oh what a tangled web we weave
When first we practice spin
Where all truth's misrepresented
And lying is no sin

No longer reading black or white
Just multi shades of grey
And nothing's really what it seems
Words don't mean what they say

I'm really quite surprised at YOU
I thought you were well-schooled
Though times you'll get away with it
We won't ALWAYS be fooled!

We all thought you were clever
While you thought us naïve
It seems you can't be trusted now
Your word we don't believe

So spin and spin great Spinning Top
Today you've lost control
What profit then to gain the world
If you should lose your soul?

It is a tangled web we weave
Of that there is no doubt
But know my friends that all your sins
Will surely find you out.

Poets In The Pink

~ The Taxi Driver Poet ~

EVERYBODY'S DOING IT!!

Anglers do it with their floats
Sailors do it in their boats
MPs do it all for votes
Journalists do it just for quotes

Writers do it with a pen
Gay men do it with gay men
The PM does it at Number Ten
So Cherie must do it - though God knows when!

Nationalists do it wrapped in flags
Transvestites do it all for Drags
John Prescott does it in two Jags
Mandy does it with Brazilian fags

Lawyers do it inside court
Hookers do it if they're bought
Clare must do it too (Clare Short???)
Well pardon me but . . . Stuff that thought!

Judges do it on the Bench
Troopers do it in a trench
Mechanics do it with a wrench
And I'd do it NOW with a fulsome wench!

~ The Taxi Driver Poet ~

Drinkers do it propped on bars
Golfers do it all by pars
Drivers do it in their cars
Groupies do it all - for stars!

Astronomers do it in the night time sky
Philosophers do it - then they wonder why
Shy girls do it even though they're shy
Pilots do it every time they fly

Soldiers do it in egg yolks
Swimmers do it in different strokes
Comedians do it just for jokes
Slappers do it with too many blokes

Canines do it on all fours
Hermits do it behind closed doors
Scrubbers do it on office floors
Adulterers do it - but they might do yours!

Grandad does it when he wears Old Spice
Nice girls do it - if you're REALLY nice!
Call girls do it if you pay the price
Pop stars do it - even Baby Spice!

~ The Taxi Driver Poet ~

DISPOSABLE PEOPLE, DISPOSABLE LIVES

Disposable forks and disposable knives
Disposable people, disposable lives;
Throwaway cups and throwaway plates
Throwaway partners and throwaway mates;
Chuck-able bottles with chuck-able lids
Chuck-able fathers for chuck-able kids

Disposable people - just rubbish to ditch:
The man is a bastard, the woman's a bitch.
Disposable people with throwaway lives
Replaceable husbands wed temporary wives.

All things are transient; so clearly that's wrong!
Nothing is permanent, nothing lasts long
You find that your life is not something you like?
Then ditch it and bin it and get on your bike!
Just find a new focus, ambition or dream;
There's horses for courses so switch in midstream

Abandon the future you promised to share
Leave soul mates, life-partners, alone in despair;
With no thought of others, it's always you first
'mongst bitches and bastards you folk are the worst.

Disposing of people like throwaway knives
Demeaning, destroying, dumped husbands and wives.

~ The Taxi Driver Poet ~

Rejecting your partners, replacing your mates
You throw away dreams like disposable plates

Disposable forks and disposable knives
Disposable people, disposable lives;
Throwaway cups and throwaway plates,
Throwaway partners and throwaway mates;
Chuck-able bottles with chuck-able lids
Chuck-able fathers for chuck-able kids

Disposable people - just rubbish to ditch
You're trashing the treasures that once made you rich
Disposable people with throwaway lives
The sell-by date passed for ex-husbands, ex-wives
Disposable people, disposable lives
Throwaway cups, saucers, plates, forks and knives.

All things are temporary, so who can you trust?
Your future betrayed in a moment of lust
You promised forever but you've had enough
Your partner exchanged for a new bit of stuff.

Disposable forks and disposable knives
Disposable people, disposable lives;
Throwaway cups and throwaway plates
Throwaway partners and throwaway mates;
Chuck-able bottles with chuck-able lids
Chuck-able fathers for chuck-able kids.

Poets In The Pink

~ The Taxi Driver Poet ~

AN INCH UPON A MAP

It's just an inch upon a map
And a visit's so worthwhile
But any man she's tried to send
Has missed it by a mile!

A sacred inch upon a map
If men knew what to do
It's the Gateway to Heaven
But they haven't got a clue!

It's just an inch upon a map
A place of perfect bliss
But one that most Neanderthals
Are guaranteed to miss.

A magic inch upon a map
That men just cannot find
A scarce frequented territory
To blow the purest mind.

Not <u>just</u> an inch upon a map
It's Heaven here on Earth
And a man you've trained to find it?
What price would he be worth!!

~ The Taxi Driver Poet ~

YOU ARE THE WEAKEST LINK - GOODBYE!!

You never found my 'G' spot
And you couldn't spell foreplay
I was looking for Adonis
Found a lazy, lousy lay
YOU ARE THE WEAKEST LINK - GOODBYE!!

You've got clumsy fumbling fingers
You're a man with no finesse
You never could unsnap my bra
Or just unzip my dress
YOU ARE THE WEAKEST LINK - GOODBYE!!

You'd never heard of Tantric sex
And you couldn't make it last
You'd start things off at ten o'clock
And shoot your load by quarter past!
YOU ARE THE WEAKEST LINK - GOODBYE!!

I'd been longing for a subtle touch
And you'd grope me like a plank
Give me the choice of sex with you
And I'd rather have a ... Mars bar!
YOU ARE THE WEAKEST LINK - GOODBYE!!

~ The Taxi Driver Poet ~

WHY A WOMAN TURNS THE LIGHTS OFF
(OR WHY A MAN ALWAYS LEAVES BEFORE THE WOMAN WAKES UP)

He can't believe what's happened to
The woman of his dreams . . . .
He surveys this sleeping beauty
With barely muted screams.
He didn't think he'd been that pissed
But now he's not quite sure
And this woman lying next to him
He's never seen before!

Last night she seemed so stunning
A drop-dead gorgeous blonde
But in the night some wicked witch
Has waved her ugly wand.
Had she but kept the lights on
In that vital quarter hour
He would've seen she disappeared
When she stepped in the shower.
First she shed her hair extensions
Then pad by pad her bust
And slowly she dismantled
The object of his lust.
Then she used her normal shower-gel
Which "refreshes night and day"
But this time it had a special touch
And it washed her tan away!!
And though she'd spent an hour or more
Painting it in place
She then applied this facial scrub
That would remove her face.

Poets In The Pink

~ The Taxi Driver Poet ~

But the lights were off, the room was dark
When she slipped into bed
And the vision of her loveliness
Still lived . . . inside his head!
But the room was dim (and so was he!)
And lager fuelled his lust
And he didn't seem to notice that . . .
She'd lost her hair and bust.
Well . . if he was aware of it
He didn't seem to mind
As two were one in passion
And their bodies intertwined.
(and of course) he felt that he had done his best
He swore he'd heard her moan
While in her head she's thinking
"this bastard better phone!"

Now, the falseness of her hair and nails
Is not what really matters
But in the cold harsh light of day
His dream-girl lies in tatters
And so he did the dirty deed
He'd done so many times before
He silently slipped-on his clothes
Then he bolted for the door.
But his final act of cruelty
As he sneaked through her hall
The **bastard** took his number back
To make sure she can't call!!

Poets In The Pink

~ The Taxi Driver Poet ~

WITHOUT YOU . . . . .

Without you, life would be like an omelette
    Without a hint of Dijon
Without you, the world would be full of horses
    That we couldn't ride upon
Without you, would be like trying to make
    sandwiches without a loaf of bread
Without you, there would be no point of getting out
    Or IN to bed
Without you, we wouldn't need calendars or clocks
    There'd be no point in time
Without you, life would be devoid of reason and my
    Poems wouldn't rhyme
Without you, I'd tour the pubs and clubs
    Yet never find a bar
Without you, a Peugeot 306
    Is just another car
Without you, I'd never hear Rice Krispies going
    Snap, and crackle, pop
Without you, there'd be no reason
    To shop until I drop
Without you, bees would know they can't fly
    And they'd stop making honey
Without you, banks would open even less
    And rob us of our money
Without you, we could have a million suns and still
    It wouldn't be sunny

~ The Taxi Driver Poet ~

Without you, comedians would forget their jokes
    And no-one would be funny
Without you, there'd be no reason to start
    Or end my days
Without you, we'd have an onion sandwich
    But not the mayonnaise
Without you, all kinds of pleasure would lose
    Their sense of fun
Without you, then sexual games would be games
    Best played by one
Without you, I could win the Lottery
    And then stick it on the fire
Without you, (even God would miss this angel
    From His choir)
Without you, the birds would find they have
    No voice for singing
Without you, my telephone just needn't
    Bother ringing
Without you, I might as well just work
    Without a wage
Without you, the words I write would run
    And leave the page
Without you, my world just wouldn't
    Ever be the same
Without you, I would be dead
    In everything bar name

~ The Taxi Driver Poet ~

Without you, I wouldn't ever find myself
    In so much trouble
Without you, there'd be no-one whose pin could
    Burst my bubble
Without you, life would be one of those awful,
    Nightmare dreams
Without you, a giant bag of REVELS would be full
    Of orange creams
Without you, is a tiny phrase but its emptiness
    Immense
Without you, is quite intolerable in past, or present,
    Future tense

Without you,

    I wouldn't have a hope
    I wouldn't stand a prayer
    I never, ever would arrive
    I'd never quite get there
    I'd spend my whole life searching for
    The happiness I'd lost
    My skin might feel the sunshine but
    My heart would know the frost

    Without you

~ Louise Ashley ~

'Bird On A Wire'
Perched on a nest of humour, Louise exposes fact and fantasy from any situation she considers worthy of dissection. Poet, creative writing tutor, editor of Living Poets Magazine, mother of two and domestic engineer; she performs at theatres, festivals, café bars, and private and corporate events. Her work has been published in numerous national and international magazines and many anthologies. Her latest book Angels In Asda reaped success when her poem Recipe For Life was featured by Sarah Kennedy on BBC Radio2.

Random Facts (in her own words): I wear boots in summer, I collect words not paperweights; I hate beer, shell suits and gherkins. I love old fashioned roses, my children and my husband . . . . although I may possibly leave him for Mel Gibson! Other interests include playing the guitar, music, yoga, sculpting, renovating a VW Camper Van and of course, WORLD PEACE!

Poets In The Pink

~ Louise Ashley ~

WHEN DID YOU STOP LIVING?

When did you stop living?
When did the sentimental gifts transform
Into small grocery items like bread and milk

The heart-shaped chalk board
Hanging -next to the fridge,
No longer declares undying love,
Just bullet points:

- Razor blades
- Conditioner
- Stuffing

Dining out and dancing compromised
For a home movie and bucket of popcorn.
Where's the enthusiasm, vision, passion?
Laughter was compacted into tablet form
And was swallowed up
Like the pound in a supermarket trolley.

I suspected this was merely existence
When the eye contact spiralled down
That same critical day
You were afflicted by
One
Word
Answers

I lie in this skin, a sacrifice
But will not surrender to this code of life
This soul will not be boxed
This world will stop to draw a breath
And then . . . .

Poets In The Pink

~ Louise Ashley ~

BITE

Skin
Fashions
Lust within
Eve's crisp temptation
Bursts
Collects morning's due -
Fallen
Bruised
Not so
Golden
Delicious
You

~ Louise Ashley ~

IN BED WITH A POET

A pillow of verse softens
All previous dawns.
He strokes conversation with
Complimentary words.
Although worlds apart
Music of poetry stretches
To each shore.
Islands merge, encounter discovery.
The mystery of communication is solved.
The language of love embraces
Couplet through metaphor,
Spoon feeding sentences
In verbal seduction of the heart.
Vowels taste like freshly baked bread.
Breath is tapered to a whisper.
The voice shapes mood
And rhythm in the delicacy
Of a Petrarchan Sonnet.

~ Louise Ashley ~

PEEL ME OFF THE CEILING

"Undress from the waist down,
Leave your socks on" she said.
I scented a surgical smell
As I lay nervously on the bed.

A quick wipe over, then with spatula in hand
She pasted me with precision;
Knowing what I know now
It should be banned!

Well you could have peeled me off the ceiling
When this sadist let rip.
Her dulcet tones echoed:
"Full Monty, or just a landing strip?"

Confused by all her questions
And the sheer intense pain,
I tried to give an answer
But my voice gave way to strain.

As she pushed my leg above me
I yelled "I think I'll pass!"
"Lie back!" she commanded, "I've nearly finished!"
And tore a strip off my ass.

~ Louise Ashley ~

Just when I thought it was all over
And could have danced a sleek Lambada,
She clenched a pair of tweezers,
I clenched my teeth much harder.

"It won't be long now sweetie,
You just need a little pluck"
I wiped the tears from my eyes and cheeks
And thought oh for God's sake let me go duck!

She deflected all resistance,
Slapped cream on skin now red and numb,
Rubbed her hands together,
Smiled, and said "There, all done."

Considering a holiday in the Seychelles?
Be very, very wary!
Forget that thong bikini
That won't give way to hairy.

Heed these words of warning:
If shaping eyebrows makes you beg.
Just get yourself a wetsuit
And take your hols at Skeg!!

~ Louise Ashley ~

SUN GODDESS

Sun Goddess
Stands motionless
Soaking up
Her pale distress
In a tubular grail
Of loneliness.
Sacramental
UV caress
Lacks that certain
Exotic finesse.
Worshipping
Oblivious.
Melanoma
SOS,
The penance
Of this ritual chess.
Solar light
Celestial dress
Sun Goddess
Lies motionless.

~ Louise Ashley ~

SEMPER FIDELIS

They left me letters,
Bound in, brown paper.
No string, held together with pride -

He strolls into the story of a starry night,
Writes with wild colour of highlands.
Speaks of forever, Glenn Miller, sketches thistles and Lochs.
Captures the heart of his country, says "Darling".

She poses in silk headscarf with an "English Rose" smile
Before lasting texture of dry stone walls,
Green woven landscapes, clear blue of sky and lakes.
Seals this, not so black and white impression,
Sends it, enveloped with love.

The past fades timelessly into present.
Holding this bundle of words,
Recalling how they once, accounted for me;
Just as precious and preserving.

They signed off each memoir "Semper Fidelis"
I walk through a pine-scented forest of thieves,
Steal your heart and remain,
Yours, forever faith-full.

~ Louise Ashley ~

SILENCE

Silence stills this moment,
To a frozen pitch in time.
Nurses drip emotion,
Shuffle lives,
Quietly unfold pristine linen.
Distant voices
In clean corridors fade.
Leaning into vacant air
I strain to hear your breath,
Kiss your forehead.
Lips blister with disbelief.
An awkward numbness paves my skin,
Time will not thaw its hollow touch.
In this soundproof cubical of cold
Life is muted and all that's left
Is the incredible volume of death

~ Louise Ashley ~

THE FAMILIARITY OF YOUR KISS

The familiarity of your kiss
Holds me,
Shapes these lips with security.
The familiarity of your kiss
Soothes this mouth
With sweet memories.
The familiarity of your kiss
Still echoes the lips of a stranger.
The familiarity of your kiss
Reassures me,
This face curves and chimes
This smile rings out your name.
The familiarity of your kiss
Is total bliss.
The familiarity of your kiss
Is missed,

        But the taste still lingers.

~ Louise Ashley ~

STRAWBERRIES AND CHAMPAGNE
(NO COMPROMISE!)

I wanted strawberries and champagne
You gave me Twiglets and Lambrini
I would have compromised
With Milktray and Martini

I wanted Paris in the Spring
You gave me Morecambe in November
I would have compromised
With Salcombe, on any date I could remember

I wanted an orchestra of music
You played the naff ring tone on your phone
I would have compromised
With a humble melody of your own

I wanted candles and poetry
You lit up, read me the latest score
I would have compromised
But I think football is a bore

~ Louise Ashley ~

I wanted passion and roses
You channel-hopped and stunk of Brut
I would have compromised
If you'd stuck the match on mute

I wanted dining out and dancing
You made me lasagne á la microwave
I would have compromised
But I'm really not that brave

I wanted Mel Gibson
And all you gave was you
I won't compromise
So I'm sorry - but we're through!

~ Louise Ashley ~

LITTLE DEVILS

At morning's break, they wake,
For one more hour I'm wishing.
At day's first light, they come to life
To find their prey is missing.

They search with haste, as they give chase,
Each bed they find uncovered.
I try to hide, they're by my side,
I fear I am discovered.

These creatures climb, they crawl, they whine
They never show me mercy.
When they are cruel, obey their rule,
They're worse unfed and thirsty.

They wreck my home, I can't condone
Their rampage is perfection.
As day creeps on, their wicked fun
Plays tricks on my affection.

I look at them, but can't condemn
Their naughty acts of mischief.
For as night draws, I have good cause
To sigh and reap my relief.

When fast asleep, I take a peep
To find these 'Little Devils'
Have closed their eyes, put on disguise
To look like 'Little Angels.'

~ Louise Ashley ~

BEYOND THE IRONING PILE

Fists clenched
Standing over
Sssssteaming boxers,
She jabs at arms and legs,
Crosses cuffs and collars.
Bounces back and forth
On the rope
Flattening unsuspecting nylons.
In singeing heat
Squeezes, releases
Annihilating the creases.
In this material maze
She uppercuts the haze,
Realises time IS pressing
And feeling cornered
Throws in the towel,
Floats like a butterfly
Into unexplored sky.
No longer in denial
Discovers - there is LIFE
Beyond the ironing pile!

~ Louise Ashley ~

DEATH BY TV

You create your own reality,
Sit before your square god
That suggests
How you live your life,
Programmes your emotions.

Cocooned with cushions
On sofa islands,
Boring husbands
And wives
Lead repetitive, robotized lives.

Complain when the pain
Becomes too much to bear
Revert to the almighty box
With nothing else to compare.

Turn on to death by TV,
But don't criticise me -
You carry on looking through your
Dirty, distorted lenses.
I'll stick with my rose-coloured glasses!

I will seize beauty and truth,
Harness the good in this world
And live in eternal poetry.

~ Mark Gwynne Jones ~

Mark Gwynne Jones is a poet whose surrealistic stories and Tolkienesque tales are delivered in a manner akin to theatre. You have before you a bard, a busker and a storyteller. His black humour and twists and turns of narrative make him a favourite in venues where most poets can only dream of surviving, let alone subduing the crowd to an attentive hush. Drawing on an ancient tradition, his captivating and slightly mad, mind-altering poems tackle the complexities of our changing world with a beautiful and savage humour. He lives in Derbyshire.

Poets In The Pink

~ Mark Gwynne Jones ~

ALL TANKED UP!

I want to drive a Sherman Tank
down to the shops and maybe the bank
to buy some bread and a can of beans.
I'd park on top of Mrs Muldean's people carrier:
a Ford Galaxy in sexy purple,
mounted by my lusty turtle!

I want to drive a Sherman Tank
at six o'clock when the roads are jammed.
With my head through the turret
and the radio on.
I'd be crushing cars one by one.
'Cos you might have got a brand new Porsche
or something bigger like a 4x4
but the roads are full
the roads are blocked
and a Sherman Tank can drive on top!

I want to drive a Sherman Tank
with the supergun fully cranked
and the girls gazing up in awe.
Never again would I be ignored, no!
Sat astride that giant tool,
whistling the tune to Battle of the Bulge.
The girls would implode in fits of goo
as I gave them a wink and rumbled through . . .

~ Mark Gwynne Jones ~

I want to drive a Sherman Tank
to demonstrate my decadence.
Out along the Boulevard
I'd make boy-racers think their cars
silly by comparison.
And if anyone dared to overtake
I'd turn the supergun and wait
until they were 15 miles up the road
(laughing at their turtle jokes)
before the punch line made them groan,
in a burning wreck of twisted chrome.

Yes I want to drive a Sherman Tank
'cos knives and clubs make me pant and
shake and
      sweat with
           fear
and stabbing someone face to face is
hate
    full
       horror
bull-at-a-gate primitive
compared to the executive action of a 77mm missile.
Road rage, eh?!
It'd be so much easier in a Sherman Tank.

~ Mark Gwynne Jones ~

And eventually when the public twig
and Sherman Tanks are really big
and every trip to the shop and back
rattles and clanks on caterpillar tracks.
I'll leave them to their earthbound mess,
take to the air in a Harrier jet
and enjoying the space of our heavenly dome
feel like the first

    car on the road . . . .

        car on the road . . . .

            car on the road . . . .

~ Mark Gwynne Jones ~

WAKE THE DEAD

If my poems
could wake the dead
I wouldn't bother
reciting them in graveyards,
or over ancient tombs
where the grass grows large.

Nor would I bother
gesticulating
before a funeral hearse,
or upon its bonnet
climb to scrawl
a resuscitating verse. No!

I wouldn't bother.
I'd let the procession pass . . . .

And if my brother
were to suddenly die,
Recite a poem - quick! they'd cry
And would I? Would I?
          Would I hell!
No, fly brother, chime that celestial bell.
Go as gentle rain and split the light
into seven shades of which the night is woven.

Poets In The Pink

~ Mark Gwynne Jones ~

But if my poems
could wake the dead,
I'd write them on the bridges of the M25
in luminous paint so day and night
people would stop, leave their cars
and wander over the sidings.

Night and day.
Suddenly alive to the whispering grass
and the muffled laughter of clay
pretending to be dead.

~ Mark Gwynne Jones ~

Plastic Man

I knew a man
who lived within
a disposable plastic Sainsbury's bin
bag.
The whole affair was very sad
he was a plastic man
he was a plastic man

A plastic man will last forever
with a plastic mac
in the clement weather
of an indoor shopping superstore.
No he never steps outside the door.
He's a lazy, hazy, instant gravy
polymer daisy plastic man
he's a plastic man

Plastic man loves to spend
on plastic goods that never end.
He's got a plastic car, a plastic life
a plastic lover and a plastic wife
he's a plastic man
he's a plastic man

Intercourse and Super Bowl,
does them both by remote control.
Loves to watch and eat the telly
loves to watch and eat the telly?
believe me when you see his belly.
He's a rubbery, blubbery, not very cuddly
plastic man
he's a plastic man

Poets In The Pink

~ Mark Gwynne Jones ~

Wrapped in rubber he loves to dance.
Sweats inside his plastic pants.
Whips it up into a trance
of Narcissism's withering glance
(in the mirror on the wall
the mirror there sees it all).
A polymer dream that's so inflated,
his love was squashed - and laminated
he's a plastic man
he's a plastic man

You can bend him back but he won't break.
He's a plastic man make no mistake.
Woodworm, mildew, dry-rot, rust
have no fear of blue-eyed bugs.
Impervious to wear and tear
this man could last for a thousand years!
But just for fun, everyday
he seems to get - thrown away
he's a plastic man
he's a plastic man

Now in years to come, as time goes by,
and archaeologists scratch the veneer of lies
and everyone needs an oxygen pump
(in paradise by the rubbish dump)
perhaps they'll wonder upon their knees
who did wrap each slice of cheese?
And say with awe across the land:

Verily it was the plastic man

Poets In The Pink

~ Mark Gwynne Jones ~

HELICAL STAIRCASE

Is this déjà vu . . .
or have I been here before?
said the admin clerk on his way to work.

Is this that experience, where
one side of the brain is slow tomato ketchup
pounded by a boy
onto the chips and peas of realisation,
or have I been here before?
said the drunk in the café
to the lavatory door.

The helical staircase is made of glass
and beneath our feet we see our passing selves.

Do you come here often? she said.
And her voice hung
like a jet plane
scoring a line on the dome of the sky.
If it cracks we're free . . . said I.
And it made me think of the lost balloon.
It made me dream of the face
of the moon we never see.
And she said, What do you mean:
if it cracks we're free?

Poets In The Pink

~ Mark Gwynne Jones ~

The helical staircase is made of stars,
DNA and water that twists
and turns
        round
and down
        the drain.
Wanting out
but returning as rain.
As souls return, again and again.

The clown, the judge, the terminally ill
daddy inside the eyes of the girl,
the bank clerk thumbing endless notes,
the turtles keeping you afloat,
is this déjà vu?
is this déjà vu?
is this . . . that experience, where
one side of the brain is slow tomato
ketchup
pounded by a boy
onto the chips . . . .

Or have I been here before?

~ Mark Gwynne Jones ~

ORANGE GIRL

I fell in love with an orange girl
her hair plutonium blonde.
At night she slept on a solar bed
until her skin was bronze.

More than bronze, it was orange.
She was orange,
                  radiating heat.
Beside her other girls were dull,
cold and incomplete.

I fell in love with an orange girl
bright as marmalade.
At night she slept on a solar bed
and dreamt in vivid grey . . .

Dreams of love for who she was
instead of how she looked,
but in the humdrum morning rush
the dream it was forgot.

~ Mark Gwynne Jones ~

She wore Chanel, a vacant air
the poise of Harpers and Queen;
I fell in love with a girl who read
enlightened magazines.

The Perfect Man, a 10 Point Plan,
To Bulimia and Beyond . . .
the fresher, thinner you was found
singing down the john.

I fell in love with a girl who was
more than a day-glow pink.
Even marching Protestants
would shield their eyes and blink.

She was 3 Mile Island, the after glow,
a lobster boiled alive
rescued from the cooking pot
and dressed in Calvin Klein.

~ Mark Gwynne Jones ~

I fell in love with an orange girl,
she was the planet Mars,
tripping round electric suns
in a hire purchase car.

I bought her from the beauty store
where beauty is exchanged,
then took her out to show the world
and put my friends to shame.

I fell in love with a girl who freaked
for the DJ's helium love.
How you should have seen her dance
upstairs at the Paradise Club!

Voluminous and luminous
her silicone boobs did bounce
like two Belisha beacons
that held me in a trance.

~ Mark Gwynne Jones ~

I fell in love with an orange girl
bright as marmalade.
At night she slept on a solar bed
and dreamt in vivid grey . . . .

Dreams of being sold a lie
by MTV and Vogue,
a vision of perfection
that left her feeling old, bulimic,
suffering from melanoma
and decidedly . . . .
   . . . . orange.

~ Mark Gwynne Jones ~

CUCKOO IN A CLOCK

"I don't know where the day's
gone" she sighed;
as if surprised not to find it in the drugs
cabinet. Or having a bath, perhaps,
with the water

hot. But of course
it never was. The day had indeed
gone. In boxes carried by the dustbin men
out towards the edge
of town, ready

to be buried with yesterdays.
It disappeared, like that golden orb,
over the urban horizon. Taking with it
the birdsong she never heard,
the sunlit brook

~ Mark Gwynne Jones ~

she never saw and a cool
breeze. Fleet of foot and swift of soul
it passed this way an hour ago.
It tiptoed round you whilst you read
and turning to the door

left. Burning up
a flight of stairs
three streets and an afternoon
before you even knew. Funny, because,
when you did know

and watched it through
the office window,
it sat on its hands and pretended to be going . . .
nowhere, but,
cuckoo in a clock.

~ Mark Gwynne Jones ~

THE NATTERJACK TOAD

'Twas either spellbound or mesmerised
the Natterjack Toad - with eyes
like glass - unblinking.
No twitch of the tongue could tell
Whether or not the toad was even thinking!

There it lay,
staring at the sky.
Day
    after day
as if waiting for a fly . . . .
But, the Natterjack Toad was in no hurry. No.
She was stuck to the road by a passing lorry!

Yes,
the Natterjack Toad would never go far.
A fact confirmed by the 4x4 Mitsubishi
    with fuel injection
        powered steering
            digital radio
                alloys
and an LPG conversion
        just to show
how much you care.

~ Alison L R Davies ~

Alison is a writer, storyteller, and poet, who hails from Nottingham. Her short fiction has appeared in numerous magazines and anthologies in the UK, USA, and Australia. She also writes non-fiction articles which have appeared in a number of on-the-shelf magazines in the UK.

Sarob Press published her first book of short stories Small Deaths in May 2003, and her dark fantasy novel King of the Birds is due for release later this year. In addition to her published work Alison has a great love for Storytelling and you can find her performing each month at Ye Olde Trip to Jerusalem, along with other members of The Storytellers of Nottingham.

Alison has written many performances pieces (stories & poems) for adults and children, does work in schools and also has a regular Writers Workshop slot on Radio Nottingham. Her current projects include a new collection of horror stories, a selection of stories for children, and teaching materials for an educational publisher.

Poets In The Pink

~ Alison L R Davies ~

LOVE ALL CONSUMING

Love all consuming she said.
..... As she sliced off the top of his head!
Said "if you leave me I'll die."
Tell me, was that the truth or lie?
I know that you cannot respond
As you're trapped by passion's tight bond.
I know that you want to deny,
As I lean in to gouge out your eye.
But darling, don't fret so with guilt,
For your poor severed neck, it will wilt.
You see I have the true upper hand
(removed with a saw, like I'd planned!)
But I'm a woman of compassion, you'll see
If you're good, I might have you for tea!!

~ Alison L R Davies ~

SUMMER THAT WAS

"That was the summer that was," he said;
Face torn by the past.
A memory born from baking heat
And love that didn't last.
He sat before the glowing fire
His words scorched by the flame.
"That was the summer that was," he said,
"I never knew her name.
She followed me to Nottingham
On jewel encrusted feet.
She danced, she danced her vixen ways
Then left me incomplete.
And warnings? Well," the old man paused.
" I turned a stony ear.
Foolish in my arrogance,
The price I paid was dear.
With bleeding mouths we sipped red wine
Upon the Castle wall,
Stained by drunken residue;
I never knew I'd fall.
Teasingly she led me on
Past fountain, square and slab;
Ice cream coated lips cajoled,
Each word a gentle stab.
Then, slipping icy fingers,
She chilled my sweat-soaked palms.
Beneath the warm and honeyed skies
I bathed in all her charms."

~ Alison L R Davies ~

The wily fire cast a glow,
A splinter of sunlight.
"That was the summer that was," **he said**
Reproachful to the night.
"A sultry, endless summer,
So balmy and extreme;
But always follows winter's truth:
Reality comes keen.
I looked for her, I searched for days
All drizzle worn and grey.
But sludge transformed those grassy paths
And washed her shine away.
And now I find I'm lost again
Beside old Guy Fawkes' fire.
Sweet summer had her wicked way
Then tossed me on the pyre."
He frowned, the amber caught his eye
His smoke choked tears dissolved
"That was the summer that was," **he said**
"but now she's left me cold."

~ Alison L R Davies ~

TREE MAGIC

Roots rip through my aching spine,
A tingle of memories, rough and wild;
The steady pull of sentient time and
I am feral, nature's child,
Unkempt, at ease in woody arms.
Spindle fingers catch each breath.
I drink the pungent cedar charms,
A bitter quaff of sap still fresh.
And whilst I wallow in regression
Kept in hollow leafy gaze,
Well aware of life's impression
Filtering the green soaked haze.
Tree majestic, token spirit;
Magic steeped in scaly form.
In your boughs there is no limit
To the power man has drawn.
Yet you stay here in the madness
That we call the modern world;
A single icon drenched in sadness,
Joints still crumbling, branches curled.

~ Alison L R Davies ~

ON RAVEN WINGS

Black is nothing in your eyes
The call is pastel sweet.
I watch - I stand, my heart belies
The patter of your feet.
I am bewitched; I do not dare
Your eyes chastise me more.
A single feather cuts the air,
A mocking, spitting caw.
In legends old they speak your name,
A hushed and whispered sound;
The ghastly and forbidden flame,
A dream to which I'm bound.
You stalk the tumbling tower walls,
A familiar shibboleth;
Prelude as the demon falls
A never-ending myth.
Oh Raven skin, Oh Raven fair,
I stand before your tree;
My wishes, should I care to dare,
Then . . . . .
         would you grant them me?

~ Alison L R Davies ~

FRAN

Gingerly she greets the day
From her makeshift bed,
A crumpled tabloid duvet,
A plastic bag to lay her head.
The bile of the night before
Is rising in her throat
Countless shots of cheap whisky
Blot out the past and stain her coat.
The coat, the one she borrowed
On a period of short term lend
Is from the local bin man,
Her one and only human friend.
Snags run along the hem line,
An elbow peers out from the sleeve
But still it hangs together
With determination to match her need.
Francesca's what they call her,
A tag that once labelled her salubrious life.
It's hard to believe when you look at her now,
She played the role of an officer's wife.
Pride took her down initially,
Never one to reach for a hand.
They said he was killed in action;
The words carefully formed and suitably planned.

~ Alison L R Davies ~

The child died, rejected;
Her body consumed and withered away.
The money vanished much faster,
Survival by will from day to day.
The years, like carriages upon a freight train,
Rolled by without time for a chat.
The lines drew their pattern along her forehead,
So now she's took to wearing a hat.
"She's crazy," they whisper, "she talks to herself"
The rumours spread fast on the streets.
Fran merely smiles her acceptance,
Accustomed to the hostile strangers she meets.
Pigeons and sparrows shuffle close to her feet,
An old mutt happily trots at her side.
Immediately at ease she takes comfort,
With these friends there are no secrets to hide.
She'll spend the last years of her life in this way,
Making a home where she can;
Desperately longing to be taken,
Reunited with her man.
When they find her sleeping the eternal sleep,
Surrounded by cast outs and strays
Tell me, who will light a candle
To signify the end of her days?

~ Alison L R Davies ~

LOVE

So caring you change to suit my needs
Clothing me in understanding smiles
Sometimes I wonder - are you real?
Or am I trapped in daydream for a while?
And really, would it help me to move on?
To cut my losses, heartstrings, sweet adieu?
I swoon beneath the blanket of your words
Remembering the feeling that is you.
Yes love, I've got the measure of you now.
For how can this denial be complete without
A sombre feeling of regret?
Without the tempting passion of your heat?
Goodbyes, they skirt the edges of your face.
Like question marks you want me to retract.
But always I am yours, a willing slave.
Love has me and it will not give me back.

~ Alison L R Davies ~

STOLEN

It seems that in the lingering days
With sunlight trapped in glittering haze
The seasons shifted, wordless dreams,
And you were gone, or so it seems
That in the cluster of the years,
Of balmy nights and countless tears,
Of chasing, catching, holding close,
You went away, became a ghost.
And for all the time that's past,
The splintered memories, broken glass,
While inspiration purged my soul,
Sweet life itself from you was stole.
The dream I harboured - it came true,
Do you recall I shared with you
The remnants of my old ink pen,
The poems, I changed some of them.
The drawing rendered from your paints,
The glossy colours, now dusty flakes.
You titled it to complement
My work, my heart, the time we spent.
Oh but it is a thousand years
Of secrets kept and conquered fears,
Of stories, and there are a few
Intoxicating moments too.
And all the empty spaces filled
The faces change, the contents spilled
From hearts and minds that must move on.
A life is stolen. You are gone.

~ Alison L R Davies ~

QUEEN OF THE UNDEAD

Take me,
Cool yourself within.
Chill the stone that killed your heart.
Consummate my sin.
Follow me into the mire,
The smoke is calling you.
The voices that live in your head
Provide a different view.
Open up to your desire.
Open up a vein
For I am the Queen of the Undead,
A gift to all insane.
My life will never give you hope
But it will bring relief.
Swallow, go on, swallow deep
The blood of true belief.

~ Michael J Kaye ~

Michael Kaye was born and raised in Huddersfield, West Yorkshire.

He currently lives in Forest Fields, Nottingham, where he writes poetry and prose.

He has worked as an English teacher in both Leicester and Nottingham but now runs Creative Writing workshops for children and for adults.

Email: michaeljkaye@ukonline.co.uk

Poets In The Pink

~ Michael J Kaye ~

HONEY JAR

The jar is half full, set honey
Dissolves into the suds, warm water
Rinses the bees sugar away,
Sediment trickles down the pipe into
The drains, out of sight, out of mind.

The label is scraped off, the glass
Filled, then emptied, filled then emptied
Until, it's clear, until it sparkles with an
Emptiness that fills it to the brim.

The pollen that contains the flower
The honey that's full with the
Hum and buzz of the comb,
Hive and bee are surrendered,
Giving way to tides of nothingness
That flood the jar and spill over
To engulf us.

~ Michael J Kaye ~

HOW LITTLE, HOW LITTLE I KNOW

Why this pain when a football
Club from your home town goes down?
What is a home town?
Why do you always say yes
When asked out?

Why do you sleep in late
In the summer?
Why this sore throat
After a first kiss in many months?

Why do you read these books,
Highlight these lines, make notes
In this book?
What is being stored?
What to keep?
How much should be discarded?

Why contemplate other options -
Writing, psychology, enlightenment?
What is the ego made of?
Why, after all these months, does
The drive, the discipline slip?
Sloth? Apathy? Indifference?
A deeper understanding?

Why even bother with these thoughts?
Why such self awareness?
Why worry about what others might think?
(that's a useful question, surely - if you

~ Michael J Kaye ~

Don't know the workings of this mind,
How can you speculate on others?)

Why bother to stop and shake the hand
Of the beckoning drunk?
Why walk these streets, those hills?
Why not roam this mind?
Get lost in its deceitful landscape?
Its infinite spaces, the dense undergrowth
Of its gnarled and entwined forests?
Map out those contradictions, note those
Places.

Why not be underwhelmed
By infinitude?
Allow the contrariness to confuse,
Let it lead you everywhere
Before it takes you nowhere.
Watch it, note its workings,
Its subtleties, its delusions
Without comment,
Without judgement.

Why not watch it,
Passionately,
Detachedly
And see what's there
When it's given its all
And you're still watching

What then?
What then?

~ Michael J Kaye ~

PYROTECHNICS OF THE HEART

Climbing above Kentmere
Drawn to the mountain top
Breathing effortlessly striding
Squelching through bog
Pulled along, driving on

These hills, the copper stain of bracken
The grey sea, beyond
Windermere below
Shade and light
Fill me with awe
But there's more, infinitely more:
You are here too, within
And when I feel your presence
This heart swells under your pull

Its high tide, surging, rising to the tug
Of the moon
Until I'm in your orbit
Spinning with energy
Revolving - striding along
The globe turning under my feet.
I cannot resist - I let the pull
Take me and you become
The blue flame under the pan
The glowing embers beneath the log
The moon rising behind the fells
The cascading sparks, shooting high
From the night.
The boot to the ball

~ Michael J Kaye ~

The dog to the bone
The ear to the phone
From which your voice
Trickles, honey sweet honey
Dripping into my head,
Flooding my heart.

As I slide with the shale
Run with the beck
Splash through the marsh
See the three deer bound off,
I am full with this
Reservoir full

Pulled inextricably, joyously
To you,
The same force that draws
The gaze to the sky
That turns the leaves to russet
All as irresistible as the smile
Which cracks this fool's face
And I roll on, stepping where
I have to go.

~ Michael J Kaye ~

SONG OF NOTHING

In the beginning there was
Zilch
Sweet FA
Diddley squit
Nowt
Not a sausage
No happenings
To rub together
Bugger all

No - thing
No - one
Zero
Nothing
Emptiness
A vacuum
A hollowness of infinitude
Absolutely nothing
Carbon
Hydrogen
Space
A void of eternal potential

From this no-thing-ness came
Every-thing

~ Michael J Kaye ~

Came
This universe

This mind can never
Comprehend
This vastness and
This energy
The nothing
Behind it all
Maybe I should give up,
Understand the futility
And give up, flow with it,
Submit.
Let it carry me away.

We come from space,
From nothing
And grow from this universe
To become earthbound.
Our blessing and our curse.
A seed germinates and sprouts
No-thing nurtures it
It begins in
A void and grows on this earth
Calcium, iron, zinc, hydrogen,
Bacteria, ions, protons, protein,
Fat, blood, bone, cells, sinew,
Atoms, particles, molecules,

~ Michael J Kaye ~

Energy
This is all these bodies are
They come from no-thing
They return to no-thing.

Not knowing my own mind,
I'm clear in my confusion,
I see through the glass of my delusion.
It's unfathomable, as infinitely
Perplexing as the universe
To wander through it is to
Enter a world of metaphor
In which nothing is as it seems,
In which, of which, I know
Fuck all.

Explosions, implosions, sparks
Of feeling, of thought,
The words that label this
Hate, that love
This good, that bad
Only add to the entanglement:
The twisting vines of thought,
The buds, the leaves of feeling
And, just as that grows from the earth,
We stretch out towards the heaven,
The skies, the space from whence we came,
Moon,

~ Michael J Kaye ~

Sun,
Stars.

But I don't understand this:
The earth is a world of distraction,
Of energies that pull, push, tug,
Squeeze us into other places.
I feel all this as
I walk
Through Galway
With this mind,
This libido which fills
Me with
Empty yearning
For the women I see.
But all it is is energy,
The love I have for comradeship,
For everyone I know and don't know.
A love
That comes
From
No-thing.

~ Michael J Kaye ~

WHERE IS HE?

He sees your laughter - it's
Glowing orange, radiating
Into him
He says you're blue when
You dance, that he hears
You on the wind which
Blows into him

When he nips and
Licks your
Neck, he tastes the ocean
And, next, he's jumped in to
The swirling waves of you.

He goes deeper, as low as
Your navel where his tongue
Tingles from the touch of silk
Silk he'll wrap himself up in

He drinks - slurps your scent
So he's drifting, roaming away
Over hills and valleys
Hills and valleys

~ Michael J Kaye ~

Until he's full,
Wearisome with joy which
Sparkles and tumbles
Through him

The diamond of vodka catches his eye
A gift accepted, taken by tongue
Off your lip
He swallows it and it becomes
Lodged between his ribs

Touch it! - see!
- I'm only telling it how it is
Hungry tongue, greedy hands
Which explore like he's
A blind man with a
3-D map, the contours
Of a land he's never visited -
And
X marks the spot.

~ Michael J Kaye ~

EXCESS BAGGAGE

Baby, baby, this carousel has stopped
The baggage-handler's worked till he's dropped.
If you would kindly make your way to the plane's hold
You can collect your own luggage, your wheelie cases
Rucksacks, beach bags, backpacks,
The designer garbage, dolce gabbana, hazelnut, sultana

We apologise for the delay but have no fear
It's time to take responsibility for your own gear.
A case labelled pride has spilled its guts on the ramp
Another, sexual hang-ups, is rather damp.
One has slipped its strap, lost its noose
A crate of fear has worked its way loose.

Those with excess baggage must declare
The origin of the hang-up, or leave it there,
Where specially trained dogs will sniff it for odium
And our caring officers will prise it open.
One abandoned case has been found
Dumped in the toilet as if to drown
So if any one is missing hope
Will they please join the queue
You've been here so often, you know what to do.

Will the Premiership footballer who's lost his phone
Shut the fuck up - you don't know you've been born -
And gather up your designer gear
And shove it in the testosterone case

Poets In The Pink

~ Michael J Kaye ~

Along with the boasts of spit-roasts and 5-in-a-sack
This is your last flight - we don't want you back.

In the spirit of less is more, those with the lightest of loads
Will pass through now - this is the crack:
First class passengers, and those with golf clubs
Can you kindly fuck off to the back?!
Will the boozers remain seated for another glug
Whilst anyone with a laptop knows where to stick the plug

A controlled explosion will blow away
All packages of violence and moral decay
A cluster of cases, each labelled hate
Is rotting away, next to Hell's gate
For those swollen with pomposity too heavy to lift
Here's a sharp prick, take it as a gift
And those who drag along heavy sacks of ignorance
May leave them by the fire
Drop the load and watch it expire

Massive duties will be paid on baggage
That roots you in the mire,
On excess luggage, that prevents you getting higher.
In a change of policy those whose vanity,
Riches and superiority
Exceed the allowance, will be grounded then hounded
Till they learn to let go
For only then baby, will the carousel begin to flow.

Poets In The Pink

~ Michael J Kaye ~

PUNCTURE

This is the bike ride that crosses the borders
Between opaque ice and personal disorders
    The silence between us is glazed and brittle,
    Like fickle drizzle, as clingy as mizzle.
We ride out, astride these bikes, gliding
Two planets that collided, now anger subsiding.
    Like snooker balls - attraction matched by repulsion
    Love to hate, hate to love, clarity to delusion
We ride on inflated spheres, round and round,
Alloy and rubber, chewing up the ground.
    A coin will spin until it drops
    A bubble will float until it pops
And once more, we've reached a juncture
That can't be patched like a puncture
    'Cos I aint got the repair kit, I'm lacking the glue
    Get off the bike and push, what more can we do
There's hawthorns at work, the tyres are spiked
And all is as still as the pike, stoned, silent beneath ice.
    A hole gets patched, a hurt heals and this is the deal
    Grabbing the barb is hard, so let's be real -
Finding and removing the thorn will offer solution,
And turn wheels iced with their own confusion
    Revolutions from trails of delusion, snarled in mud
    Into the by-ways of happiness, the avenues of love
We must extract the thorn, cycle these spiky miles
And see just how easily holes fill with smiles.
    So, go on admit it, you've got nowt to hide
    You, woman, are the thorn in my side.

~ Michelle 'Mother' Hubbard ~

Michelle is a poet, storyteller, African drummer, and active community member born and based in Nottingham.

A founder member of BLACK DROP, which offers a platform for local black performance artists to explore their abilities and talents without the conventional restraints of "A4 double-spaced" mentality. All types of expression are welcome and encouraged, from poetry to rap, song and storytelling. It is an exhilarating and intoxicating mix.

Michelle has performed on Radio Nottingham and made many guest appearances at various launch events. Her poetry draws its influence from wide and varied sources, ranging from the African folk tales of Anansie, to the "golden cloths" of Yates, the romance of Keats, and the wit of Benjamin Zephaniah - who she just happens to be pen-pals with!

Poets In The Pink

~ Michelle 'Mother' Hubbard ~

STANDING OUT IN A CROWD

He was nothing much. Plain.
Until you looked again.
Looked a little deeper into eyes
Focused with a darkness of cool coals
Placed amongst hot flames.

He was nothing much. Ordinary.
Yet something most extraordinary
Was extra special about him.
He, who blended in, yet stood out in a crowd,
Like the moon amid stars.

He was nothing much. Nothing.
Yet somehow I saw everything.
Everything I had ever dreamed of,
Though never imagined could be possible,
Like meeting my Maker and living to tell the tale.

~ Michelle 'Mother' Hubbard ~

THE TRAVELLERS PRAYER

Our Captain, who art in the heavens
Hallowed be thy name
Thy destination come
Thy will be done
Abroad as it is in Heaven

Give us this day hotel and bread
And forgive us as foreigners
As we forgive those
Who are foreigners against us

And lead us off into temptation
But deliver us short of evil . . .
. . . . . And men!!

~ Michelle 'Mother' Hubbard ~

I'M LEAVING

Part one: our yesterday -

In the kitchen, chopping pumpkin
You watch, and touch my skin
I prepare its firm orange flesh
Your hand touches my breast

In the centre, seeds lay waiting
You need more than 'giving-taking'
I season the soup, and it sure smells fine
Your DNA is embroiled with mine

Part two: today -

Raw. Unprepared
The items for today's meal
Sit on the chopping board
Still in the carrier bag

Where's dinner? They ask
Where's my sanity? She mumbles

They look at each other, frowning
Reach for the biscuit tin
She looks at her heart, crying
Reaches for her coat
Closing the door behind her
For the last time

~ Michelle 'Mother' Hubbard ~

MIND YOUR WORDS

I walked round town
Words and sounds
Stuck to the sole of my shoes
I stepped in a pile of words
And some seeped through
There was
- or is it "there were"
Verbs, nouns and pronouns
Some words I couldn't pronounce

Some of them were obscene
I tried to scrape them off
You know,
Casually, before anyone could see!

Some of them got stuck in the treads
- I trampled them home with me
Trod them into the pages of my poetry

Some needed clarity
I sought the dictionary
Then, not knowing what else to do
I deliberately stamped on a few!

People just throw their words anywhere
With no thought for others at all

~ Michelle 'Mother' Hubbard ~

So many words go to waste
Disregarded
Misplaced

I found some real beauties!
I'm saving them in a jar
For the right moment

Each verbal component
Will be carefully selected
And then eloquently projected

Please don't throw your words around
Cluttering up the streets and towns
You don't know the untold damage they'll do
Stuck to the soles of the wrong shoe

UNTITLED

We honeymooned
But never married
  We had two children
  Both unplanned
We shared the house
But not the mortgage
  We talked to each other
  But never listened
We separated
And never looked back

~ Michelle 'Mother' Hubbard ~

BIRDS EYE VIEW

The people
The steeple
(all equal)
The churches
Paying homage
Women rummage
Through purses
And handbags
Dreaming, of glossy mags,
Of wedding gowns
And historic towns

The quaint little village
With its people
And its steeple
The church
With its porch
And candlelit torch
Cold grey brick
Where moss grows thick
And the ageing smell
We know too well
Of the people
The steeple
The church

~ Michelle 'Mother' Hubbard ~

And beyond the porch
Stands a silver birch
Where birds gather
And twitter
Their Sunday morning service
We hear this
As they sing
Of Spring
And the people
And the steeple
And the church
And the porch
With its torch
And the silver birch
Upon which they perch
From where they have
A perfect view
And they listen
To the twittering
Amongst you

~ Michelle 'Mother' Hubbard ~

ALL WOMAN

I lay black lace upon my skin
It kind of expresses the mood that I'm in
NO - I'm not doing it for him
But to remind myself-

I'M ALL WOMAN.

I am full of sensuality
Bursting with creativity
Gracefully blessed emotionally
And most of all -

I'M ALL WOMAN.

I am proud of my feminine qualities
And of these I'll make no apologies
Bodily curves
Whatever the figure . . . .
Don't want it smaller
Don't want it bigger

There's a deeper side to me
Sit and listen, quietly
I allow myself to be,
Whatever I want to be
And whatever that is -

I'M ALL WOMAN!

~ Michelle 'Mother' Hubbard ~

THIS LUSTFUL AFFAIR

I lust after you:
Chocolate.
Cake.
And biscuits.
And each time I swear,
I'm ending this affair!

But I need you
On my tongue,
On my lips,
Then you sink to my hips
Hanging heavy
You do this to me

You're first on my list
I cannot resist,
Your sweetness -
You are my weakness!

I cannot refrain,
I want you again
And again.
AND AGAIN!

And so I remain
Locked in this affair
Because,
When I need you,
Any time, any place . . . .
You are there!

~ Michelle 'Mother' Hubbard ~

THE HUMBLE OASIS

Chilling in the backyard
Of an inner-city terrace
Council tax, long overdue
There's no view
But, today the sun is shining
So we're relaxing. Unwinding

Up above, pigeons coo
Perching, on broken guttering
Moss forests burst through
Every crack 'n' crevice

Tall, dark green wheelie-bin
The urban backyard centre-piece
Who needs deckchairs
When kitchen chairs rock
Backwards and forwards, rhythmically
On cracked uneven concrete surface

Overflow drip, drip, drips
Forming small damp pool in one corner
Sparrows drink,
Grateful of the incidental water feature

Pebble dashed oasis
Creaking gate squeaks, like chirping crickets
And this concrete haven
Dispels my myths of the Mediterranean

~ Michelle 'Mother' Hubbard ~

MY BOX OF BRYANT AND MAY

The neat, petite
Rattling box
With its one edge smooth
And the other,
Coarse and rough
Just enough
To ignite
Like dynamite
The long thin fragile stick
With the Fuchsia-pink icing tip

One deliberate swift stroke
It hissed and it crackled
With flame and smoke
Tantalised by the scent
Of a match, spent

Oh, the sizzling Sulphur

Wizened, blackened, charred remains

Box
Matchstick
Friction
Flames

~ Michelle 'Mother' Hubbard ~

BEE STINGS

Enjoying the sunshine
We picnicked on the grass
As he flew past
Robust and proud
In his loud
Yellow and black
Stripy velvet jacket

An outburst of laughter
(which wasn't aimed at him)
Stopped him dead in his tracks
About turn. Full steam ahead
Back in our direction
With an angry expression

At first, we ignored him
But he was pushing for a fight
We tried
To duck and dive
The lemonade spilt onto the sandwiches
He complained louder and angrier
Someone trod on the cake
  - and it isn't over 'til the fat man stings!

~ Michelle 'Mother' Hubbard ~

Hot under his thick velvet collar
Hanging heavy and out of shape
Drunk on nectar
He went for the attack
We decided to fight back
Arms flapping
Tea-towel flicking

He saw an opening
Charged right in
Plunged his sword through the delicate skin
Someone screaming, crying
 - the fat man is stinging!

PRAYERS IN THE DARKNESS

In single solitary silence
I lay awake and pray
Not so much out of belief
But for fear of being alone
And it keeps me company

~ Michelle 'Mother' Hubbard ~

LOVE'S MATURITY

I listen to the silence
And I understand him
I smile at the words
He doesn't speak
I'm warmed by the hand
That does not need to touch me
I peer into his eyes
And I still turn weak

I'm safe in the arms
That don't have to hold me
My lips wear a kiss
That we shared long ago
He spares on emotion
Yet I know he loves me
His heart holds my heart
And it never lets go

He watches me quietly
Hoping I'm not looking
Responds to my moods
Like a sailor steers the seas
He doesn't give me flowers
But he gives me my space
And he never tries to change me
But allows me to be me

~ Ian Collinson ~

Ian has been performing his poetry at live 'open mike' events around the east midlands for a number of years. A founder member of Living Poets, he writes a regular column for their magazine. He believes that poetry today has become marginalized because too many practitioners accept, even welcome, a small press approach, giving public readings in an atmosphere resembling a lecture theatre rather than live theatre. He feels strongly that lessons should be learned from performances poets and that all poetry worthy of the name demands to be delivered with a fluency and energy that engages the audience on a physical and emotional as well as a cerebral level. Only by doing this can poetry rediscover its voice and re-engage with its long lost public.

Ian lives in Nottingham. Recently unmarried, he has two young adults that he calls children. His spare time activities include running, sailing and managing a print business.

Poets In The Pink

Poets In The Pink

~ Ian Collinson ~

I WISH I COULD WRITE LIKE A WOMAN

I wish I could write like a woman,
Pulsating with passion and rage.
But my words are as cool as cucumbers,
They just lie there inert on the page.

I wish I could write like a woman,
My lyric would leap from the heart.
But I am all mouth and trousers,
Obsessed with the wrong body part.

I wish I could write like a woman,
And my verses electrically arc.
But I am as dead as a Dodo,
A plug that refuses to spark.

~ Ian Collinson ~

CONVERSATIONS WITH MY DAUGHTER

She sits there, head averted
And thumbs out another text.
A secret smile greets its reply
While she begins the next.

The hissing Walkman headset
Always guards her private space,
And the telly in the background
Is another hiding place.

Could we progress beyond
A sullen grunt or two?
I don't need conversation
Monosyllables will do.

She's got to check her email
If the world-wide web is free.
Her messages go everywhere
To everyone but me.

~ Ian Collinson ~

And then I have a brainwave
I say, look it's getting late.
I'll go and make some dinner
You can shunt around your plate.

I hurry to the kitchen,
Try to text a line or two:
How r u sweetie pumpkin?
Don't frgt ur Dad lvs u.

And so I stand here waiting . . . .
This is taking quite a while . . .
She's probably composing . . . .
Some sweet thing to make me smile.

She bursts into the kitchen
Her eyes are filled with hate.
I've selected the wrong number
And sent it to her mate!

~ Ian Collinson ~

ONE FOOT IN THE RAVE

I'm gonna book a holiday
I fancy something flirty
But I don't think I can get away
With Club 18-30.
I wanna dance 'til half past three
And drown myself in lager
But all the agents offer me
Is packages with Saga.
They've got lots of destinations
But they're not the ones I need.
Can't believe my generation's
Going to Berwick-upon-Tweed.
Don't wanna do a coach tour
Or a long weekend in Rhyl
Let me Salsa on the dance floor
Of a nightclub in Brazil.
So if you're listening Saga
Please stop sending me junk mail.
I'll ring you when I'm gaga
And my senses start to fail.
You can save that week brass rubbing
For the sober senior set.
I've still got to do some clubbing
So I won't be joining yet.

~ Ian Collinson ~

NUTCRACKERS

You think you'll keep your nuts intact?
They're probably already cracked!
Nutcrackers are not sweet these days,
They've dumped ingratiating ways.
Our fruiting bodies go to waste,
All ground-up into almond paste.
You may think you've done all you can
But they'll still end up marzipan.

Many times a bloke has boasted
When he's already dry roasted.
Beware these vigorous jeunne filles
They'll get a grip on your brazils.
You might not feel the slightest pain
But you may never walk again.
And it is not good policy
To try to wrench the buggers free.

There's just one hope for you and me
They might get a nut allergy.
Their power will go down the drain,
If they can no longer nuts contain,
And bags of nuts will be set free
To swing in peace and harmony.
And cries will echo through the land
That nutcrackers should all be banned.

~ Ian Collinson ~

INTELLECTUAL

I'm an intellectual, baby,
Could think you into outer space.
But you won't get my attention
If you're just a pretty face.
Don't bother with seduction,
Or flaunting body parts.
It's semantics that excite me
And the philosophic arts.

I'm an intellectual, baby,
I'd be top of any class.
Got facts at all my fingertips
Got brain cells in my arse.
I mesmerise opponents
With my sophistry and zeal.
I can run rings round anything
So long as it's not real.

~ Ian Collinson ~

I'm an intellectual, baby,
I slice and dice with life
And fillet out its mysteries
Just like an old fishwife.
For things are so much simpler
If you carve them into pieces,
Discarding the uncertainties
That bugger up your thesis.

I'm an intellectual, baby,
I use brains instead of brawn
And I can share my knowledge
Boning up with you 'til dawn.
I may not be a He-man
But nobody thinks I'm weak.
It's only when they kiss my butt
I turn the other cheek.

~ Ian Collinson ~

SOME OF MY BEST FRIENDS ARE ANSWERING MACHINES

My Nokia does not vibrate,
My voicemail is bereft,
My inbox is a wilderness,
Nobody sends a text.

My ansafone lies dormant
No one calls up any more.
Readers Digest competitions
All I get through my front door.

I've got more connectivity
Than missions to the Moon
But nothing is incoming,
All my systems seem immune.

I am excommunicado,
No new messages for me,
Though I am always calling
With my O2 minutes free.

~ Ian Collinson ~

You can't get to the phone, right now,
You can't get to the phone.
You really cannot answer it
Though you must be at home.

It's not that you don't want to
It's just that you cannot.
Conversation with your message
All the intercourse I got.

I know I should be patient and
There's others in the hunt.
I guess it's not the best thing
Yelling: "call me back!" . . . so blunt.

So now you know my story.
No new messages for me.
Just junk mail through my letterbox
And spam on my PC.

~ Ian Collinson ~

NEARLY BELOVED

Nearly beloved,
Blight of my life,
Personification
Of trouble and strife.
We were not incompatible,
We could succeed.
I'm sure I remember
One time we agreed.
How could I anticipate?
How could I tell?
That your maison d'tre
Was D.I.Y. hell.
Such savage high standards
Forbid any fun.
You want to redo it all
When it's just done.

Nearly beloved,
Blight of my life,
Your only mistake
Was becoming my wife.
In all other respects
You're infallibly right,
My worthless opinions
Must shun the daylight.
For I am Neanderthal
Stone Age and lost,
Suspended forever

~ Ian Collinson ~

In your permafrost.
We battled incessantly
Love ran away
But love didn't live
To fight another day.

Nearly beloved,
Blight of my life,
You put our relationship
Under the knife.
I struggled my hardest
To make things come right.
Your iceberg obstructed
I crashed in the night.
I moved to a flat
With wallpaper I hate
But one thing is certain
I won't decorate.
I sit writing poems,
My language is lush
My pen will be mightier
Than your paintbrush.

~ Ian Collinson ~

LADY OF THE RINGS

She's got rings on each finger
And lots on her toes
And I keep losing count
Of the ones in her nose.
She's punctured in places
You wouldn't believe
With sleepers in spots
That would make some folks heave.
The tongue thing's a challenge
The navel's ok
But moving down further
Well, shall we just say
That some of her rings
Tend to get in the way.
She's got more bits of metal
Than creatures on farms.
When she goes into airports
She sets off alarms.
Don't misunderstand me
I think she looks smart.
You could say she's hooked me
And pierced my heart.
But one thing perplexes me
'til I am enraged.
What on earth will I give her
If we get engaged?

~ Sue Allen ~

Sue is a curvaceous woman with attitude. This is reflected in her poetry, which focuses on her experience as a woman whose dress size is outsized, with a mind to match. Her work runs the gambit of the emotions, from the cuttingly funny to the profoundly spiritual.

Performance poet, freelance writer, workshop leader; she IS so much more than the sum of her bra size. She loves creative and imaginative people, angels and crystals; hates bananas, straight lines and men in grey suits; and is a sucker for anyone who can play acoustic guitar.

Her work has been published in numerous anthologies and magazines, and she has recently co-authored a book with friend and fellow poet Louise Ashley Angels In Asda. Sue is always working on her next poetry adventure and is currently completing a project working with people with dementia.

Sue has an honours degree in Applied Social Studies and is a qualified social worker. She lives and works in Nottinghamshire.

Poets In The Pink

~ Sue Allen ~

MEN ARE LIKE BRAS

Men are like bras,
They start off firm
And supportive, giving
Form and foundation to
Your life.

But soon they start to lose
The point, turning into
Grey and saggy
Threadbare reflections
Of their former selves.

The material falls into
Holes in your hands,
As you contemplate the
Ultimate disappointment
Of elasticated passion.

Let down and droopy
Just when you needed some
Uplift in your life.

Let that be a lesson to you girls -
Never trust anyone
Who says:
       "cross my heart!"

~ Sue Allen ~

LOVE IN CINEMASCOPE

Take me through the mirror darkly.
Let me see the other side of you,
Reflected in a broken pane.
Pieces of your face,
Lying in shards across the
Cutting room floor;
Like a shattered matine idol's dreams.
I recall the glamour shot that struck a reflection,
Then ricocheted off the walls in silver backed illusion.
I remember the heart-throb who haunted my
Young girl uncertainty, giving me false hope
In insipid movie kisses. Leading me to the final reel,
Only to disappear, when the house lights go up.

The walk home is illuminated in fake orange tan,
And the dark glass is waiting behind
The dressing table make-up,
For us to step forward into centre stage.

~ Sue Allen ~

I'M ONLY A GIRLIE

Don't tell me I'm only a girlie
I'm stronger than you think!

I can break your heart with one flick of my hair.
I can make your ceiling sink.

Don't tell me I'm only a girlie!
I don't accept that 'macho-man' crap
I won't fulfil your ego trip,
Of pregnant and tied to the tap.

I hold in my power re-creation,
My body is mine to possess.
I don't need your heart-felt approval,
Of how I should look, eat and dress.

Don't tell me I'm only a girlie,
That I need to be cared for by you.

Why should I accept your hang-ups
Of what I should say, be or do?

Don't tell me I'm only a girlie!
Who are you to set out my plan?

Don't tell me I'm only a girlie -
After all you're only a man!!

~ Sue Allen ~

HEARTLESS

I gave you my heart to keep,
And you lost it.

You said it was
Around here somewhere,
With all the other things you didn't need.

You looked under the bed
And found a broken fragment
Distorted by dust,
Another, pricking at the back of your mind
And another, clinging to the sleeve
Of the red sweater you bought me for Valentines.

You tried to fix it back together,
Hoping I wouldn't notice the cracks.
But even superglue couldn't get us
To stick it out.

When I said I was leaving,
You said I was heartless.

But not quite,
I carried enough in my bag
To start again.

~ Sue Allen ~

I WANT TO BE STING'S ACOUSTIC GUITAR..

I want to be Sting's acoustic guitar.
I want to feel his tender, strong fingers
Travel up and down my spinal fret board
As we dance.
I want to be so close I can hear
Every breath he takes.
I want to match every move he makes,
In that one tantric moment of his embrace.
I want to inspire his creativity
As we walk in fields of gold;
The steel of his eyes
Reflecting our connection.,
Melting into my own rainforest
Of lacquered desire
As he strums a love song to life.

And I am content.

~ Sue Allen ~

YOU PAINTED ME IN PALE, PALE BLUE

You painted me in pale, pale blue
So I wouldn't show when the background went in.
You wanted me to fade like first love in the rain.
You wanted me to wane into your memory,
A triumph of Mars over Venus.
What planet are you from
If you think losing you could make me disappear
Into the wild blue yonder?
You forget, I too have a paintbrush
And the power to paint the universe
Stars and all.
I can leave you out on Pluto, where you belong
And take my chances with a new stargazer.

~ Sue Allen ~

GREEN HOG DAY

My green heart is melting
Spreading like the bile of a bastard day
Across the rubber-backed upholstery of my boyfriend's car.
Slow sinews of hope,
Sliding into cracks and crevices
Like jelly-mould emotions left too long in the sun.
Creeping into corners of doubt,
Where even the hot-rod with steam-propelled penis envy
Cannot force it free.

Why does this always happen to me?

Why does the lid on my emotional emulsion
always dislodge itself just when I think
I've avoided that particular sleeping policeman?

Why do I always wake-up
Only to find that I've run over him again
And again
And again the paint is out of the can.

~ Sue Allen ~

BROKEN DREAMS OF BETTER PLACES

My duvet took me prisoner
Seducing me with promises
Of warmth and security.
Hypothermic hypocrite
Bursting with duck-down disappointment.
Hypnotically snuggling into my body
Lulling me into sleep with
Broken dreams of better places
Promising pain-free endings,
Like an aspirin and vodka overdose.
Just close your eyes and let time
drool from the corners of your mouth . . .
I wake.
Leaving damp despair on my pillowslip;
Breaking free,
To search for hope
In caffeine and cornflakes.

~ Sue Allen ~

BLACK ORCHID
(in memory of Nina Simone)

Black orchid,
Rare and exotic bloom
Forced through the cracks of concrete racism
Singing your songs in black velvet tones of blue,
You speak to my bones
I echo in the arc of your voice
Each song a melody of joy and pain
Don't explain! Don't explain!

~ Sue Allen ~

COLLISION COURSE

The shortest distance between two points is a straight line

But you caught me on the curve
Sending me into a spin
Like a leaf in autumn,
Slipping and sliding along the track
Losing my grip.
Unable to gauge the depth of it
I gave myself up to the ride.

LOVE ---- that non-stop train of thought
Whistling through the night,
Rocking away into the distance,
Like a promise
Unfulfilled.

Missing the points we screamed
Hoping to go faster,

Neither of us seeing the dead man breaking.

The shortest distance between two points is a straight line.

Like the stopping distance
Between your heart and mine.

~ Sue Allen ~

CIRCUS ACT

Walking the tightrope
With arms outstretched
Taking tenderfoot-steps
Without a net.

Feeling the tension in my body
As the balance shifts.

She who hesitates has missed.

Rushing headlong
Into a spin of hope and elation,
As I fall head-first into
The oblivion of love, faith and devotion.

With only a clown to break my fall.

I am left prostrate
On the yellow sawdust floor;
Trying to avoid the stallion's footfall
As the bare-back rider
Gallops past.
Fixing me with his
Fake greasepaint grin.

I take my bow
And leave.
Falling from the full house of my emotion
As the circus rolls on by:
Chimera in motion.

~ Sue Allen ~

ST ELMO'S FIRE

Call me email,
And tell me how Moby fares.
Does he still write songs
Of morbid fascination,
Sung in parchment voice,
Lashed to Ahab's web of
Self-destruction?

And what of you?
Do you dance defiant
To the sound of sirens,
As the great white page
Of your imagination
Dives in the storm-grey seas
Of someone else's creation?

Is your fate sealed by
Prophecy or design?

Ask the tattooed man
The meaning of St. Elmo's fire
Then make your choice:
Sink or sing.

~ Sue Allen ~

CAPTIVE BUTTERFLY WIVES

Sirocco winds
Blow across the estate,
Driven by the chaos wings
Of captive butterfly wives,
Caught in the net
Of domestic distraction.
Foiled by the lure
Of love, that brief sham of sunlight,
Redefined by moonbeam reflections,
Into promises that fade with the dawn.
Blue and white striped
Carrier bags, overflowing with
Economy priced disappointment
Anchor them to reality,
Smother their dreams of flight.
The breathless burden
Of everyday existence
Fluttering against the glass
Of the bell-jar
Slowly filling with cyanide.

~ Sue Allen ~

ISIS AND OSIRIS

The crone mourns
For the life of Osiris
Drawn into fourteen pieces
By his brother betrayed.
Isis the watcher
Waits for his
Sweet scented rebirth
When the contents of
Their hearts shall be
Avenged.
The missing phallus
Reformed by a
Maiden's hand.
The Sun-God reigns
With the ebb and flow
Of the Nile.
Only the Earth Mother
Is constant.

~ Neil F Winfield ~

Veteran musician and sometime poet, Neil F Winfield is active in organising and presenting poetry events in Derby. Neil lives in his native Derbyshire and continues to play guitar around the midlands area.

Poets In The Pink

~ Neil F Winfield ~

MAKING LOVE

She said
"You've been making love with my sister"
I said
"No, I haven't"
She said
"You have!"
I said
"I haven't"
She said
"You're a liar"
I said
"I'm not"
And turned over to sleep the sleep
Of the righteous.
Of all the times I've
Had sex with her sister
I never once thought of it as
Making love.

~ Neil F Winfield ~

GOOD WOMEN

Women come and go
As do whims and fancies
Each with aroma and flavour
That one may pause to savour
As relationship may pass from ripe to rotten
Those poor decisions, best forgotten
But she was a good woman
As good women go
And as good women go
She went.

~ Neil F Winfield ~

THE GREATEST

Who was the greatest in the twentieth century?
Was it the self-appointed Muhammad Ali?
Or the charismatic President
John F Kennedy,
Neil Armstrong, Churchill, Elvis Presley,
Einstein with his Theory of Relativity,
The Wright Brothers, Freud, Madame Curie,
Hillary, Fleming, or Mahatma Ghandi?

There are many contenders
From the marvellous to the mischievous
But the greatest were the Beatles
They were bigger than Jesus.

~ Neil F Winfield ~

MARRIAGE 1

With a long-term marriage
One has to be a diplomat
For when it's not the same old sex
You think, "Where did she learn that?"

MARRIAGE 2

I have regret
About our marriage
Even though
It was a disaster

But given a choice
About divorce
I'd prefer to be
A widower.

MARRIAGE 3

My ex-wife was a horrible woman
In fact a total bastard
For now she will remain nameless
I had her tombstone
Sandblasted.

~ Neil F Winfield ~

LITTLE POEMS

SUSPICION

Eve suspected Adam
Of having an affair
So every night when he came home
She checked all his ribs were there.

IMPRESSIONS

I had an interest in art
So I studied at the Sorbonne.
I learned that with Impressionism
I always make a good first one.

LUNATIC

I phoned the police station today
It wasn't a question of death or life
I wanted to see if a lunatic had escaped
'cos someone's run off with my wife.

~ Neil F Winfield ~

MORE LITTLE POEMS

DRINK

I love drink, drink, drinking
But I'm not an alcoholic
'cos I drink until I vomit
Therefore I'm bulimic.

POLITICIANS

Politicians promise better days
When they're up for ballot
But each time they're elected
I find their fingers in my wallet.

PETS

There are too many domestic pets around
I've a solution for all that
Make cat food out of dog
And dog food out of cat.

~ Neil F Winfield ~

MORE LITTLE POEMS

MAN

A man he will be happy
Until a woman takes his heart
He will do anything she wants him to
And then he'll fall apart

WOMAN

A woman is like a wheelbarrow
This I won't forget
She's difficult to push around
But easy to upset.

DOGS

Some say that dogs are intelligent
Some say dogs are thick
But how many other animals
Can train a man to throw a stick?

~ Neil F Winfield ~

MORE LITTLE POEMS

ROCK OF AGES

Rock of ages
Shelter me
From my ex-wife's
Tyranny
I pray that fortune
May grant me luck
She gets run over
By a truck.

FROM MY WINDOW

From my window
I shot a gun
Little caring where
The bullet would run
An alarm maybe
I should raise
For haven't seen
My wife for days.

~ Diane Doran ~

Diane has written poetry and short stories since childhood and kept them in a biscuit tin.
She believes that poetry has to resonate with people's real lives rather than needing translation. It has to touch you in a way that is inspirational, thought-challenging and life changing. Diane performed poetry in the early 90s, running workshops and performing at the Leicester Literature Festival. She was also part of the Trellis women's writing group in Nottingham and performed as part of the Indelible Ink series.

Diane has worked as a psychiatric nurse and NHS manager for 20 years. Although she still works part time for the NHS, she is now a partner in a property development business and company director of a martial arts supply business.

She lives in Nottinghamshire with Soulmate Paul and has two boys aged 25 and 11. She loves theatre, films, dancing and red wine - and has recently taken up Karate (ouch!).

Poets In The Pink

~ Diane Doran ~

TO WATCH YOU SLEEPING

If all I could do
Was to watch you sleeping
It would be enough.

The flicker of your eyelids
Dreams passing behind your eyes,
Rise and fall of your chest,
Soft breath across your open lips.

Seeing you, hair skewed across a single pillow
A picture of you laying across the bed
Arms bent up to your face in boxer's stance.

Each time you stir,
I would wish for you
To open your eyes
And see me there.

I would have my mind
Photograph each movement
That you make
Through one short airless night.

Without touching,
Without feeling,
Still loving,
You.

This, in truth,
Would be enough.

~ Diane Doran ~

SEXUAL TRUTH

It starts with a little kissing.
Progresses to a little fondling
Then passionate kissing.

His tongue,
Red and swollen
Thrusts urgently
Into your receptive mouth.

How exciting.

Exposing your breasts,
He gasps;
The kissing stops,
You feel flattered.
He begins the foreplay,
Strokes your undulating body.
It begins to be exciting.

You feel like Emmanuelle,
You want him to talk dirty,
You feel urgent.

~ Diane Doran ~

So he stops,
Stays silent
And smiles.

Disappointed,
You sigh,
Then remember,
This is sex.

Build in a little longing groan;
He'll like that!

He positions himself above you,
You feel premature anti-climax.

He enters you,
You're not yet wet enough. You feel pain,
And groan.
He likes that.

He lifts himself up and down;
A hard, furious rate.
Feel him laying on your chest,

~ Diane Doran ~

You can't breathe.
Push his shoulders up,
Breathe.

He bends his head down,
To suck your nipple.
Why does he do that?
You can hardly feel him inside you,
But he likes that.

His urgency becomes great . . . .
He is close to orgasm,
You are close to tears.
So it comes,
He collapsing
Onto your chest.
You can't breathe.
Kiss him,
Sidle out from beneath him.

Look exhausted,
But interested.
He likes that.

~ Diane Doran ~

PROJECTIONS

When I say:
"Are you alright?"
Secretly,
'til recently,
And unbeknown to me,
I was asking you
To ask me
How I am.

If I say,
"You look unhappy"
I want you
To notice
My sorrow.

~ Diane Doran ~

I WANT IT THIS WAY

You will bring me breakfast
On a tray with a rose
In a china white vase
In a huge sleigh bed
With white sheets of broderie anglaise.

You will kiss me
In an offhand way
Before you dress
In your Italian suit
And designer shades.

We will both be young
But experienced enough
To know what we want,
Confident in that way you are
When you're too old to care.

I decided that I will be beautiful;
I will have long auburn hair,
Eyes the colour of thundery sky
That laugh whatever my mood
And follow you always.

~ Diane Doran ~

We will celebrate each day
That we have together,
Dance slow as the radio plays,
Never wanting to remember the time
That we couldn't hold each other's heart.

We will watch sunsets together
Sipping Chardonnay from cut crystal glasses,
Playing backgammon or chess
Until the red lights die,
Sinking behind green hills before us.

I will wear white floating dresses
Of cotton and silk,
Play piano and sing to you,
And you will love me forever
Because you know that this will never come again.

~ Diane Doran ~

DISTANT INFANT

My eyes don't cry any more Mummy,
Your eyes brim constant with your pain
Whilst mine hides inside.

Occasionally, I cry in blood.

In school,
At my desk
Hard and wood,
I feel drips of warm
Red tears,
Falling slowly from my neck.

I touch there quickly
And feel afraid
That someone might glimpse
My bloody pain,
But looking furtive then, at my tiny hands,
There's no blood or tears.

In seeing if they notice,
I find I can see no-one.
Not even you Mummy.

~ Diane Doran ~

HELP ME, DON'T HELP ME

I hear you say
You live on a knife's edge.
When you speak to him
In the house you share,
Your words must be carefully chosen
To circumnavigate his anger,
Bridle his hatred
Of you, of women, of his mother?

It's your responsibility,
Heed it well,
For if you fail
You'll fall, flailing,
Uncontrolled
Across the smouldering razor edge,
His wrath slicing deep and clean
Into your white and tender flesh,
Laying you open,
Bleeding,
Vulnerable,
Un-healing,
Silently screaming . . . .
As he wraps your entrails
Around your head
And you
Choose
Not to notice.

~ Diane Doran ~

BLUE ABALONE

My love for you
Roars in my heart
Like the ocean
In a storm.

I want to fill your world
As completely
As you engulf mine.

I would live with you
In Paris
On poetry, love and red wine,
Watch the sun come up
And feel your heart beating
As you hold me close,
The touch of your fingers
Across my skin
As you whisper
That you love me
Forever.

~ Diane Doran ~

I want to feel you
Holding me hard,
Stroking me,
Exorcising the ghosts
That have troubled my soul.

I give you the whole of my innerness,
Everything that is me,
To hold in the palm of your hand,
Fragile as blue abalone,

I'm trusting you
Not to hurt it,
Not to crush it,
Not to lose it.

~ Diane Doran ~

TIP TOP, PUCKA

Tip top, pucka mate,
And I'm a northern monkey.
This thing that started out so cool,
Is heating very gently.

You took me all round Harrods mate,
And to the London Tower;
I, confused about your talk,
Your mood so dark and dour.

I had all that with a man before,
I vowed not to go there again . . . .
So we went up to St Paul's Church,
And shopped in Petticoat Lane.

Then you returned to how you are,
All was bright and good and fun;
Don't know if I can go the distance,
Don't know if you want to run.

Then I wonder when you visit,
Or call me on the phone;
Because I'm not sure if I really care
Or if I just don't want to be alone.

~ Andy Postman ~

Andy Parkinson is a thoroughly nice man - and one of the most interesting and multi-talented people you are likely to meet. Writer, artist, puppeteer, street entertainer, you name it - Andy Postman is it!

Whether appearing on the folk circuit, biker rallies (wow! There's a brave man!) or wherever, Andy's work is crafted and accessible, zany and brilliant, and well received by all.

Poets In The Pink

~ Andy Postman ~

THE ABC APPLIED TO ME
(OR THE ABC OF INSANITY)

And actually Andy's abnormal - a
Brainstorming babbler, batty, bonkers, brainless booby.
Certifiable, crazy, cretin, crackpot, cracked, cranky clot.
Different-ly diagnosed, dotty, daft, dizzy, dope.
       Deluded, depressed,
       Defected, demented, deranged.
Extremely erratic, eccentric, extravagant
Foolish, funny, fixated, frustrated, fathead, frantically frenzied.
Gone - giddy - gormless.
He's hallucinating, hysterical, hyped, hypomanic
Ignorant, inattentive, insane, illogical, inconsistent, imbecile
Jittering, jumpy
Kinked.
Look! Loony, ludicrous, loco, loopy
Mind-muddled, mad, mentally-ill, manic, melancholic, moronic
Neurotic, nebulous neurosis, nervous, nutty, nincompoop
Odd, ob-sessed
Potty, peculiar, paranoic psychosis, psychopath,
- Queer -
Raving, rushing, retard.
Strange - scatty, suicidal, simpleton
Thoughtless, thickhead, twisted, touched
Uncontrollable, unreasonable, unbalanced, unhinged
       Unthinking,
       Under the doctor
       Under sedation -
Vacant, void, volatile, violated.
Witless, wacky, wild, weird
X tremely X files
YYYYY you you you you you
ZAP!! Scared you!

Poets In The Pink

~ Andy Postman ~

MONTY DON (to the tune Jolene)

She'd a crush on Alan Titchmarsh too
But when she caught a sight of you
She fell in lust with you - Monty Don!
Monty Don, Monty Don, Monty Don, Monty Do-o-on
Please don't take her just because you ca-a-an.

Yes Monty Don! - with his devilish charm
Has done our marriage loads of harm
If Monty was aware of the adulation he'd got
He'd rush right round here with his dibbler -
To furrow her plot.

Monty - Monty - Oh Monty, MONTY!
She loves that Monty Don
Full Monty's what she has in mind
She's full on Monty Don

Since she's seen him on the box our relationship's ill-fated
Now all erotic dreams she has are Monty Don - imated
She fantasises about Monty in a flower garden picturesque
Tall and naked Monty - Manly - Monty-pythonesque!

MONTY! MONTY! I hate Monty Don!
Dressed in bondage rubber wellies
With his bleedin' duffle coat on.
I HATE him 'cos she loves him!
Because she wants him desperately
What's HE got that I haven't got? (besides personality!)

~ Andy Postman ~

May a plague of slugs and caterpillars
Descend upon his garden in the night
May all life there be extinguished
By a terminal dose of blight
May all wither in the hot sun
May all be washed away by rain
So she never ever sees that Monty bloody Don
On the telly again!

Monty Don, Monty Don, Monty Don, Monty Do-o-on
Please don't take her just because you ca-a-an.

She dreams about hot sex in your potting shed
Lying NAKED in your flower bed
MONTY!!
Please don't take my girl.

You're on the telly strong and tall
While I smoke dope and do fuck all
Please don't take her just because you can.

Monty Don, Monty Don, Monty Don, Monty Do-o-on
MONTY!
Please don't take my girl!

~ Andy Postman ~

SLUG IN A WINDMILL

There once was a windmill in old Amsterdam
A windmill with a slug in -
came up a sink with no plug in
It was dark 'n' damp -he said "How lucky I am
Living in a windmill in old Amsterdam."
>(Chorus)
>I saw a slug - WHERE? There on the stair.
>Where on the stair? Right there!
>A slippy slug with slime on. Oh well, I declare
>Going yuck, yuck-ity, yuck on the stair

That slug in a windmill had a very good life
Then one day decided to take him a wife
He sang out the window how lucky I am
And wrote to Computer Dating in old Amsterdam
>(Chorus)

The agency sent him a lovely slug-ess
All made up and scented in a slimy slug dress
And oh as he saw her he joyfully sang
Then they both went upstairs for a marathon bang
>(Chorus)

Now they've lots of young slugs in a windmill of slime
The slugs everyday have a wonderful time
They sing out the window how lucky we am
Living in a windmill in old Amsterdam.
>(Chorus)

Poets In The Pink

~ Andy Postman ~

AND WHEN I'M UP I'M UP
AND WHEN I'M DOWN I'M DOWN

A manic depressive diagnosed
You're welcome to visit my pad
Beware I may be up or down
Mind-muddled, mental, mad.
>(Chorus)
>Coz when I'm up I'm up
>And when I'm down I'm down
>And when I'm only half way up
>I'm neither up nor down.

Well, you may find me queer
You may find me sad
You may find me hard to understand
It's easy mate . . . I'm mad!
>(Chorus)

Well you may call me bonkers
Or a crazy kind of lad
Nutcase, barmy, crackpot, fool
No problem . . . Coz I'm mad!
>(Chorus)

Oh the grandiose way I talk
Ten thousand to the dozen again
Marched me into a hospital ward
Because I'm mad again!
>And when I'm up I'm really up
>And when I'm down I'm really down
>And when I'm only half way up
>I'm better!!

~ Andy Postman ~

BROWN

When I was a lad I'd never ever seen
A proper sea where the sea is clean -
Each year at Skegness I always found
A sea, "not blue" but gravy browned.

Now I'd seen all those brochure pictures of exotic places
With picturesque shops, beach, holiday town.
Tropical desert islands, "All with Blue Sea!"
But at Skeg' - the sea is brown!

At Skegness the sea is brown my love
As brown as suntanned skin
Elementarily, excrementally, brown my love
I wouldn't advise a swim!

Ohh! but the young and foolish swim there
In that dismal place to drown
Sucked down by the effluent undertow,
Lost forever in a sea of brown.

At Skegness the sea is "Brown"
Yes brown as brown can be
Perhaps they should promote the fact
In tourist publicity.

"Come to Skegness where the air is bracing
You'll find your visit invigorating
We've funfair, crazy golf, ice cream stall
But our unique attraction to top it all
The jewel in Skegness's crown -

~ Andy Postman ~

The sea's not a boring shade of blue
But a beautiful Bisto Brown!"

Brown with Humber estuary silt and mud
From way up the river's reach
Pouring through the cities - a sewer-
Washing down to Skeggy beach.

Where chocolate Skegnessquik mud is revealed each day
As the Brown tidal waters recede
It squelches up between your toes
It's where the nipping and biting things breed.

In the Brown. In the Brown rippled sea
Resembling wet corrugated cardboard
Brown as wholemeal bread with bits in
A Brown creosote-y sea.

Thank God I discovered Bridlington
When I was twenty-three.

~ Andy Postman ~

EDWOOD WOODWOOD

How much wood could Edwood Woodwood chuck
Edward Woodward is a very talented ac - tor
As Callan years ago he was a spy, political benefactor
He was in that fillum The Wicker Man
They burned him in the end
Tempted by the flesh, but pure in heart - what a part!
A Christian true and good
Good true British blood, Edwood Woodwood
EDWOOD WOODWOOD EDWOOD WOODWOOD
EDWOOD WOODWOOD - a new computer game
With a real hard faced hero, with a really terrific name
EDWARDO WOODWARDO
Eddie Woody for short, or ED WUD! (just a thought)
EDWARD WOODWARD in a horror screamer
Ea-dward Wood-ward when he plays the dreamer
Ha ha he he. Hedward Woodward can play a comedy part
Hilarious in the role of a drunken old fart.
EDWOOD WOODWOOD as a baddy hard as iron
EDWARD WOODWARD Sir! - brave as a British Lion.
Good old Edwood could be on a ship, tank or plane
On an 'orse, in a car, or walking. Look! There he is again!
Edwood Woodwood!
How much wood could Edwood Woodwood chuck
If Edwood Woodwood could chuck wood?
Ed-ward Wood-ward
When he's in a Hollywood-style musical production
Using his 'ead when he's in a love scene seduction,
"Ed Ed Eddie Eddie Edwarrrd Edwaarrrd WOODWAARRRD!!

~ Andy Postman ~

Edwood Woodwood could play the part of 'any man'
Or any woman. I bet he could Edwina Woodwina.
There's not a single part that Edward Woodward won't do
I'm sure he was one of the Daleks once in Doctor Who
EDWARD WOODWARD EXTERMINATE! EXTERMINATE!
Such a fine actor - why he could play the part of a horse
And he's very good at fish of course.
He's excellent at being trees,
As Edwood Wood-wood-would be
Right now he could be playing me!
"I tell you I'm Edwood Woodwood!"
No, I'm Edwood Woodwood, Eddy Woody is me!
From good old Edward Woodward
May our screens never be free.

So!
How much wood could Edwood Woodwood chuck
If Edwood Woodwood could chuck wood?
Edwood Woodwood would, could and should
Chuck as much wood
As Edwood Woodwood could chuck
If Edwood Woodwood could chuck wood.

~ Andy Postman ~

THEORY OF EVERYTHING

Scientists for years and years have tried
To find out one simple thing -
"What's the universe made up of?"
Now at last the answer . . . . String!!
STRING!! How could string be the answer
To Albert Einstein's quest?
Can the fabric of the universe be described
As a computer model of an old string vest?
Like alphabetti spaghetti, STRING spelled out
The answer to that scientific dilemma
Which caused the scientific world
A cataclysmic tremor.
Once, Boffins said, the universe was made of
Coloured billiard balls connected by little rods
Now they say "No, it's made of string!"
The silly bloody sods!
    (I'VE GOT A G-STRING THEORY, YOU KNOW
    BUT WE ALL KNOW WHERE THAT WILL GO)
"String?" you say - just take this pill
Stay on the ward - you're mentally ill.
Spike Milligan and the Goons would rejoice and sing
For they've proved that everything is "made of string"
So I'm going down to Wilko's
I'm going to buy me some twine
So a small part of the universe
Will be - just - MINE!

~ June Staines ~

June has been writing her poetry for years and words flow most easily for her when she is inspired by actual events, emotional situations, or facts of life.

Born and bred in London, she has lived in Derby for 22years now, where she works as an assistant accountant for a local company.

An ardent walker, she loves the outdoor life and travelling the world is her favourite pastime and passion. She doesn't do postcards and holiday photos, but you're in for a treat when she stands to recite her latest adventure.

Poets In The Pink

~ June Staines ~

HEAVEN NO's

NO man, NO grief
NO cruel agitator
NO hassle, NO heartache
NO power generator
NO football fanatic
NO unfaithful traitor
NO sulks, NO rows
NO tear instigator
NO strange irritations
NO cream applicator
NO time and motion
NO movement dictator
NO crowded house
NO unwanted spectator
NO pretence, NO lies
NO sneak infiltrator
NO doubts, NO fears
NO need arbitrator

YES peace of mind
And a damn good vibrator!

~ June Staines ~

INFERNO

Our love was new and exciting
It ignited from out of the blue
Affinity, happiness and laughter
Were just some of the pleasures we knew.

For a while the world was our oyster
As we moulded like hand to a glove
We glowed and beamed with a passion
In the heat and the flames of our love.

Now dowsed with emotional blackmail
By forces that could not be damned
I shield the embers and memories
While you sap the shell of a man.

~ June Staines ~

I LOVE IT

You are so warm and so inviting
Informative, exciting
And I love it when you're writing
Your poetry for me.

                You're enthusing and amusing
                    Not confusing or abusing
              And I love it when you're choosing
                      To write poetry for me.

You're submissive, intuitive
So exclusive, not elusive
And I love it when you choose to give
Your poetry to me.

                You're applying, simplifying
                    Un-denying, satisfying
              And I love it when you're smiling
                      Your poetry at me.

~ June Staines ~

SECOND THOUGHTS

Vibrator! No man! Hey, what's this I say?

Well - maybe for a while that theory's OK

But when comes the chance for flirtation and fun

The thought in my head is a different one.

To pleasure and writhe at a human touch

With passion and lust is an experience much

More exciting and intimate than a battery toy

Feel the flesh and the rhythm of a real **live** boy

Although satisfaction's **not** guaranteed

The aim for achievement fills most every need

For varied positions and meaningful thrusts

Make a "good session" an occasional MUST

Of course, emotions like love remain on the dole

To enable one's life to stay under control.

~ Ken Swallow ~

Ken was a senior lecturer in General Studies with articles and interviews published in national journals before retiring in 1990.

He then spent more of his time writing fiction and poetry and winning a host of awards locally for written and spoken pieces.

City Lights magazine described him as "writer, poet, comedian, and renaissance man". He has enjoyed success performing in comedy clubs and recently made it through to the national finals of a competition, performing in front of Jasper Carrot.

He himself describes his poetry as "in large part, middle-brow male menopausal, and . . . accessible to a fault.

Poets In The Pink

~ Ken Swallow ~

VALENTINE

If eggs were oranges
And oranges were eggs
And spiders all had feathers
And chickens had eight legs
And Cheshire cats refused to smile
And hyenas were quite dour
And hedgehogs dashed around
At fifty miles an hour
And lions just said, "Do you mind"
If you took a stick and poked 'em
And sharks lay on their backs
And liked it if you stroked 'em
If cats could bark quite loudly
And dogs just went miaow
And you got a pint of Guinness
If you milked an Irish cow

If lemmings took a step back
And said, "No, after you"

If elephants all had trunks
Ooh, hang on, they do!

If all these things could happen
If all these things could be
It still wouldn't make much sense
If you said you fancied me

~ Ken Swallow ~

ANT

A miraculous miniature machine
An ant I've seen
Crossing my paper
    I sip my tea
And marvel at the way it can
Move with such determination
Indifferent to the fortunes,
The follies and the fate of man.
A life industrious and short
It ignores the Sport,
The National and the International News,
The Crossword Clues - and on it goes
When Tennyson "took a flower
From the crannied wall"
He remarked that
If he "could understand that flower,
Root and all"
He would "understand God and man".
I can
Relate to that.
The ant is gone
I contemplate one
Bewildered creature
    I sip my tea
Bewildered creature?
Not the ant
Bewildered creature - ME.

~ Ken Swallow ~

THE KISS

Time rests sweet
Upon the tongue
Red wine trembles
In the shining glass,
Set down by fruit
Untouched, a step away,
A look, a touch and
Nothing;
Nothing more to say.

As though embraced and filled
By morning sunlight,
Blissful and pure as April rain,
We kiss.

A feather of soft snow
Falls from a slender branch.
Ice crystals on the window
Sparkle then
Start to melt; to melt away.
A breath, a heartbeat
And nothing,
Nothing,
Nothing more to say.

~ Ken Swallow ~

CARDSHARP

He knew that she knew he had deceived.

His turn to deal,
To shuffle, cut and bid. He did.
"Now I must guess the card you save."
'This card is everyman' she thought
'This card's a knave."

"I did not mean to hurt you."

He turned the cards,
Dark suits, fortune's faces - Aces
Fading - Crowns, now less than royal red.
He put the last one in the pack.
'That's my heart," she said.

~ Ken Swallow ~

DIAMOND DAYS

Once, each day was like a diamond
Bright. Hard
Marking out our lives
So clearly
Reflecting light and shadow
Days cherished
And days wished away

Now days slip by
Like raindrops from a leaf
In April
And we enjoy the touch of sunlight
Shining briefly on each jewel
Before it falls

~ Ken Swallow ~

NOT A POEM ON THE PAGE

Buzz buzz, I'm a bee
I'm a flea
I'm a bird in a tree . . . . .

(Dammit, I can't write this stuff!
I wanna be a performance poet!)

Performance poets walk about a lot
Shout a lot
Wave their arms about . . . quite a bit
Gesticulate (in public!)
Make flourishes
Like Lancelot - in Camelot

"Oh Guinevere. Thou and I could have a merry caper.
I'm more than a verse on a piece of paper."
You what?!! To pay for the coronation
You sold my horse and replaced it with an Alsatian?
Are you taking the piss?
Sending a knight out on a dog like this?

Omar Kayham had a dog (he also had a cat - Persian)
One day, his dog was licking those parts dogs can get to.
Ali Ba Ba said, "Drat! Wish I could do that!"
Omar said,
"Give him a biscuit - he'll let you!!"

~ Ken Swallow ~

I was in a pub the other day
And I met a girl called Meg.
Said she'd like to have me 'doggy' style
And she did - she bit mi' leg!

Yes, a bit of humour - a bit of rancour
"I'm a poet, not a merchant banker."
There's a line to find a rhyme for
"I'm a poet, not a merchant banker."

People think I'm a bit . . . . .
No, don't help me . . . . I'll get it
I'm a poet, not a merchant banker,
People think I'm a bit . . . Like Bogart in
'Casablanca'

"Of all the bars in Nottingham
You walk into this poetry slam;
Don't play it again Sam
It's a poem on the page."

Buzz buzz, I'm a bee
I'm a flea
I'm a bird in a tree
You can't catch me
I'm not a poem on the page.

~ Ken Swallow ~

THE PEAK PASS ROAD

I stood upon the pedals
On the Peak Pass road
Turning the world. Breathing the sky.
Charging a spirit that knew
Somehow before the mind
How to take from over the net
A shot that was struck hard
And strike it harder back
That drove me on to run the field
And will the well-struck goal.

And now what have I got?

A hat to hide my grey hair from the wind
A stick, a lonely room
And sport upon a television screen
Though mine's a different dream
Remembering the nerve and inner sight,
That knew the ball in crescent flight.
I'm with the ghosts of team mates
Running to the centre spot
And in that dream the summer sun stops
To watch me take the Peak Pass road.

~ Ken Swallow ~

BODGER BLUES

Would it pass the MOT?
I look at my car. It looks at me.
Would I?
Memory and well-mixed polyester paste
Repairing parts that time's laid waste.
When firmly set,
Rub down. Prime. Wipe clean and feel
The flaws. Repeat and wipe again.
Reveal
Swerving contours
Of forgotten pasts, clouds in a dream,
Delta patterns of a river, once a stream
With silver zeal
Through the nip of hard rocks leaping
Now in shadowed tide, near sleeping
Drifting
Slowly to a wide indifferent sea
Unburdening itself. The map is me.
Stand here and look
Though painted over, soft inflexions
Show.
My verses have imperfect rhymes
(sometimes)
I know
I know perhaps that after all
Like Plato's shadows on the wall
Somehow not real
But transient and incomplete
Our poems and lives are counterfeit.

Poets In The Pink

~ Ken Swallow ~

THE DOT COM LOT

No Marxist dialectic
No more sovereignty of nations
Liberal democracies rule OK?
And global corporations
Life and love are lotteries
There's junk mail on the mat
"Post modernism's" pass
So now where are we at?
Is this the end of history
Or have we lost the plot?
A lonely crowd of click-on kids
      We are the dot com lot.

In a 'global village'
Yet somehow on our own
Lunching with a laptop
And on a mobile phone
Recovering from 'futureshock'
We haven't come round yet.
Scratch card cowboys, cyber cats
We surf the Internet
Designer labelled, TV cabled
Wicked man! We're hot!
That means we're 'cool', ok dude?
      We are the dot com lot.

Poets In The Pink

~ Ken Swallow ~

Weary web-site wanderers
Whose e-mail's gone astray
If the medium is the message
What's the message say?
Ozzy soaps, celebs and debs
And Reality TV
Kiss and tell the tabloids
Buy one get one free
Derrida on the yellow brick road
Deconstructing Camelot
Latter-day knight fever. 'Bored of the Rings'
    We are the dot com lot.

Liberal and digital
We are consumer man
Searching for a 'partner'
Or perhaps a pension plan
Should we ask the audience
Or should we phone a friend?
Still looking for a purpose
Though history's at an end
We searched the world wide web
And the answer that we got
"You're the human race. You're lost in space"
    "You ARE the dot com lot."

~ Ken Swallow ~

THE CYCLIST

I know the sky is there
But fix my stare
Down on a wall of grey
With each clenched sway
Moving a heavy world
Beneath my wheels
Striving, driving
Pedals round, straining,
Gaining ground,
Turning, burning,
Bloodstream surging
Urging me on
Labouring, savouring
The climb gripping
Slipping up a gear
Back arching
Aching, proudly taking the hill
And at the top the sky
And I look down while
Heavens shine
And a crown that is the
Universe
Is mine!

Poets In The Pink

Poets In The Pink